Trailblazing Women of the Georgian Era

History is a commentary on the various and continuing incapabilities of men.
What is history? History is women following behind with the bucket.

Mrs Lintott ('Totty') in *The History Boys,* **by Alan Bennett.**

Dedicated to my best friend, my great supporter,
and my ever-patient wife, Philippa.

Trailblazing Women of the Georgian Era

The Eighteenth-Century Struggle for Female Success in a Man's World

Mike Rendell

PEN & SWORD
HISTORY

First published in Great Britain in 2018 by
Pen & Sword History
an imprint of
Pen & Sword Books Ltd
47 Church Street
Barnsley
South Yorkshire
S70 2AS

ISBN 978 1 47388 605 6

A CIP catalogue record for this book is available from the British Library.

Typeset by Aura Technology and Software Services, India
Printed and bound in India by Replika Press Pvt. Ltd.

Pen & Sword Books Ltd incorporates the imprints of Pen & Sword Archaeology, Atlas,
Aviation, Battleground, Discovery, Family History, History, Maritime, Military, Naval,
Politics, Railways, Select, Transport, True Crime, and Fiction, Frontline Books, Leo Cooper,
Praetorian Press, Seaforth Publishing and Wharncliffe.

For a complete list of Pen & Sword titles please contact
PEN & SWORD BOOKS LIMITED
47 Church Street, Barnsley, South Yorkshire, S70 2AS, England
E-mail: enquiries@pen-and-sword.co.uk
Website: www.pen-and-sword.co.uk

Contents

Preface

In the eighteenth century, men had all the power and all the glory. The laws were written by men, for men. All the Members of Parliament, the entire judiciary, all the magistrates and the entire bureaucracy of government were male. A list of the rights of married women would have been a blank page. More and more, a woman was expected to retreat to the domestic arena, to provide a home for her spouse, to rear his children and run his household. Her entire education and upbringing were designed to enable her to secure a husband and to carry out her domestic duties in a genteel manner. There was no need for her to learn mathematics, or foreign languages, or be kept up to date with political and economic developments. Far better that she did not trouble her pretty little head with such matters, and instead consider how best to jug a hare or boil a fowl.

The wonder is that women put up with this straightjacket as long as they did – or that any of them chose marriage since it was little short of slavery in the eyes of the law. But a combination of factors meant that women accepted their subservient role – at least in the early part of the eighteenth century. It took time for female writers and thinkers to speak out about the injustices in Society, and longer still for men to respond to the pressure for change. After all, Mary Wollstonecraft's paradigm-breaking book *The Vindication of the Rights of Woman* was published in 1792, whereas the first female MP to take her seat in the House of Commons was Nancy, Viscountess Astor, in 1919.

It would, however, be wrong to assume that the female voice went completely unheard. This voice was drowned out by the cacophony of great male achievements which dominated the Georgian era – the birth of Empire, the ascendancy over France, and the industrialisation of the English landscape were seen as male successes. Men like Nelson, Anson, Cook, and Clive became household names. Boulton, Wedgwood, and Watt made their industrial fortunes, and they are the ones we remember. By comparison, female achievements seem pallid and unremarkable, but that is to over-simplify matters. There were achievements, in the face of extraordinary opposition and male obstinacy, and this book intends to look at some of those achievements and ask: why weren't there more? How come there were any at all? What held women back? What were the qualities shared by the women who made breakthroughs?

The concept of female inequality is all the more surprising given that England had no fewer than three female monarchs in the space of the preceding two centuries: the oft-despised Queen Mary in 1553; Queen Elizabeth (the ever-popular 'Good Queen Bess') in 1558; and the much-revered Queen Anne in 1702. Together they accounted for almost exactly a third of the regnal years of the 200-year period up until 1750. You would think that having a female ruler at the helm would have removed a few glass ceilings. Wrong – if anything it drew a line underneath their achievements and there was no significant trickling-down of female advancement, or even more importantly, any greater recognition of female capabilities.

When I started writing this book, I wrote: 'The writer is no feminist, but nor is he an apologist for male bigotry and self-interest. It happened: live with it' – but on reflection that is unjust. The story of inequality is a reminder of wasted lives caused by lack of opportunity. It is essential that we are awake to the dangers of prejudice and inequality if we are to prevent other groups from wasting their lives, ending up unfulfilled and being treated as second-class citizens. We also need to ensure that the momentum towards equality is maintained. More accurately, I would now choose to write: 'It happened: and we must all live with the consequences.'

The introductory part of the book looks at the how women were treated by the law in the eighteenth century. The main section of the book is devoted to looking at the achievements of some of the women who beat the system, to a greater or lesser degree, because they were willing and able to shift those paradigms which otherwise treated women as 'mere' home-makers and child-rearers. They were the trailblazers, who enabled later women to break down the doors of male prejudice. Of course, there were others, and some may be disappointed that different, more prominent, females have been omitted. These are simply a personal selection – not a definitive list.

****

Paradigm: noun, defined by the *Oxford English Dictionary as* 'a typical example or pattern of something; a pattern or model'.

A paradigm is an unwritten rule that things are done in a particular way, through custom or habit.

The paradigms I have chosen are:

For the Arts and Literature:
Women have neither the creativity nor flair for The Arts, outside the home.

For Science and the Scientific World:
Women have neither the intellect nor education for The Sciences.

For Business and Commerce:
Women have neither the temperament nor acumen for Business.

For Reformers and Educationalists:
Women have neither the ability nor opportunity for Influence.

'Washerwomen' by Paul Sandby.

Introduction – Women and the law

The law and customs affecting women (coverture, primogeniture, entailed interests and matrimonial causes).

COVERTURE

The law regulating rights within marriage was variously called coverture or couverture. The property rights between husband and wife were established at Common Law (rather than by Statute) and were based on the system adopted from the Norman French. The rules were largely unwritten – at least, they were never written down for the layperson to read – until Sir William Blackstone came along with his *Commentaries on the Laws of England*, published in four books in the period between 1765 and 1769. Part One dealt with the rights between individuals, with Chapter XV setting out the law relating to rights within marriage, using archaic terms like 'baron' for the man and 'feme' for the woman.

Blackstone writes:

> *By marriage, the husband and wife are one person in law: that is, the very being or legal existence of the woman is suspended during the marriage, or at least is incorporated and consolidated into that of the husband: under whose wing, protection, and cover, she performs every thing; and is therefore called in our law-french a feme-covert … is said to be covert-baron, or under the protection and influence of her husband, her baron, or lord; and her condition during her marriage is called her coverture.*

That, then, was the basis of common law in the eighteenth century – a married woman automatically came under her husband's protection. She lost her legal identity because it was totally subsumed into the identity of her husband. It followed that a woman on marriage gave up the right to sue or be sued in her own name. Her property, whether acquired before or after marriage, became the property of her husband. She was not entitled to receive a wage in her own right, because her earnings belonged to her husband.

Blackstone continued:

> *a man cannot grant any thing to his wife, or enter into covenant with her, for the grant would be to suppose her separate existence; and to covenant with her, would be only to covenant with himself: and therefore it is also generally true, that all compacts made between husband and wife, when single, are voided by the intermarriage.*

Blackstone expounded:

> *a woman can however be appointed attorney for her husband 'for that implies no separation from, but is rather a representation of, her lord'.*
>
> *a husband may also bequeath anything to his wife by will; 'for that cannot take effect till the coverture is determined by his death'.*
>
> *the husband is bound to provide his wife with necessaries by law, as much as himself; and, if she contracts debts for them, he is obliged to pay them, but for anything besides necessaries he is not chargeable.*

The effect of coverture was that a married woman, in law a *feme couvert*, really ceased to exist as a separate person. She could not enter into contracts in her own name, because all rights and obligations in any such contract vested in her husband. So if a husband and wife were in a trading partnership, there was no particular point identifying them both as individuals. In nearly all such cases, the man's name was used for all business purposes – for the shop name and on bill-heads, trade cards and so on.

Blackstone added various corollaries to his comments. The loss of individual female rights applied only to civil law – a wife could still be liable for criminal acts, but the parties could never give evidence in court either for or against each other 'partly because it is impossible their testimony should be indifferent, but principally because of the union of person'. The wife's evidence was whatever the husband said it was.

Civil law was complicated however, because the Ecclesiastical Courts had a parallel jurisdiction. These courts were completely separate from the civil courts – they had their own rules, their own court officials and their own judges, and were particularly important in cases of 'family' disputes, be it illegitimacy, marriage, separation, or custody.

Blackstone explains:

> *In the civil law the husband and the wife are considered as two distinct persons, and may have separate estates, contracts, debts, and injuries; and therefore in our ecclesiastical courts, a woman may sue and be sued without her husband.*

The chapter ends with the words:

These are the chief legal effects of marriage during the coverture; upon which we may observe, that even the disabilities which the wife lies under are for the most part intended for her protection and benefit: so great a favourite is the female sex of the laws of England.

The point was significant: coverture was seen as a shield, not a sword. It was regarded as giving protection, and many women at the time would not have seen it as unduly oppressive. Many regarded it as perfectly normal. It pre-supposed an obligation on the part of the man to provide for his wife, and she could expect him to pay for all her needs. The law may have echoed ideas of master and servant, or even, some might argue, master and slave, and certainly the language of 'baron' and 'lord' would raise the hackles of today's sisterhood. The law enshrined an inequality between the sexes, and the inherent injustice remained until Parliament eventually started to chip away at it halfway through the Victorian era.

The other side of the coin was that an *un*married woman (in legal parlance a *feme sole*) had exactly the same rights as a man. She lost her rights and her property on marriage, but she got them back on his death. This had a profound influence on female entrepreneurs. Prior to marriage a businesswoman enjoyed the full panoply of legal rights – to enter into contracts, to own property, to operate bank accounts in her own name, to invest money and receive interest and rents, to sue, and to be sued. She got back that full range of rights when she became widowed, and many of the examples of successful women described in detail in this book bear testimony to the effect that this had on women's decisions. Successful women were generally unmarried spinsters or else were widowed. It is also worth remembering that at times there could be a very considerable gender imbalance, numerically, with waves of migrants into large cities such as London and Manchester upsetting the natural order. The result: at times up to half the women, despite being of marriageable age, would not be married. *Feme sole-dom* may not have been a choice, but it certainly was not uncommon.

It has to be said that Blackstone's *Commentaries* may have had the effect of rather over-stating things. The very weight of his observations, the very rigidity of the idea of coverture, may have helped 'set in stone' something which was in fact far more fluid. The law had always been based on precedent, on case law, and the judiciary had always been eager to pick and choose which particular case to follow. This was certainly true in the Court of Chancery – known colloquially as 'the court of wills, wives and wrecks' because it dealt with probates, marital disputes and shipping law – where principles of fairness and equity were applied. This fairness often enabled married women to retain wealth through the intermediary of trustees. Without trusts, married women could not sell, mortgage, charge or lease land without the husband's consent. However, where land was held in a trust it never came under their husband's control, because it was vested in the names of third parties, i.e. the trustees.

A trust deed could protect capital from the avarice of the husband, allowing him access only to the interest. As has always been the case, where the law appears harsh there have invariably been lawyers willing to devise schemes to circumvent the perceived injustice – at a cost – and therefore the rich could often find ways to achieve their own ends. As Jonathan Swift remarked: 'Laws are like cobwebs, which may catch small flies, but let wasps and hornets break through.' Marriage Settlements and Trust Deeds were tools of the wealthy. But for 'Mrs Average' coverture meant that, to modern eyes, there was little difference between marriage and slavery. A husband might choose to give his wife 'pin money' – an allowance for her to spend on her own personal comforts – but even this reverted to her husband's estate if it was unspent at the time of his death. Wealth belonged to the married man. In return, a widow could expect an annuity from her husband's estate to provide for her old age, and the terms of that annuity would generally have been covered by the original marriage settlement, if one was ever made. Rather like 'pre-nups' today, formal deeds were always the exception rather than the rule, at least as far as the rank and file were concerned.

One example of the way the court could offer a modicum of legal rights to a wife was the case involving Lawrence Shirley, the Fourth Earl Ferrers. He inherited the title as a 25-year-old in 1745 and proceeded to sire four children by his mistress. In 1752 he married a girl in her late teens, but still kept on his mistress. A man of violent temper, with a touch of insanity and a problem with drink, he was not what the blushing bride expected. His behaviour went from obnoxious to utterly impossible. Most unusually for the period, his wife persuaded her family to pay for a private Act of Parliament to be passed, enabling her to have a legal separation. Under the terms of the separation the estate assets were vested in trustees. Rents and profits from the Ferrers' estate were to be paid to the estranged wife, with the old family steward, a man called John Johnson, acting as receiver of the rents due to her. The arrangement was a disaster, with the Earl hating having to hand control of his estate to his steward. He shot Johnson in cold blood – and the resulting trial for murder led to the Earl being dragged off to the gallows, the last peer of the realm to meet that fate. But the earlier legal proceedings did show that the courts could and would intervene, in extremely rare cases, to bypass the harsh effects of coverture.

Coverture had a few surprising consequences. It cast a shadow over criminal law – a man could not be guilty of raping his wife, because she had no right *not* to be raped by him. She was her husband's property. Coverture also meant that there was no point granting a married woman her own right to vote – because the man would control how she exercised that right. And she could have no say in how her children were to be brought up or educated, just as she had no way of separating from her husband and of supporting those children herself.

From a modern standpoint, it is this total lack of maternal rights which seems surprising – and certainly the notion of 'the rights of children are paramount' had yet to be formulated. The extraordinary case of Mary Eleanor Bowes was an example of this – the exception which proved the rule. She was twice married and had five children. Her second husband was an Irish conman who duped her into marriage on the pretext that he was at death's door. It was all a charade aimed at enabling him to get his hands on her vast wealth, and immediately the marriage ceremony was complete he made a total 'recovery'. He then set about systematically plundering her assets, while treating her with appalling cruelty, often beating her mercilessly. He was not just violent – he was a sadistic liar who would stop at nothing to prevent his victim parting him from her money. However, she eventually managed to escape his clutches long enough to file for divorce 'from bed and board' before the Ecclesiastical Courts. At the hearing before the London Consistory Court at Doctors' Commons in May 1786 she attained a remarkable triumph. Not only did she obtain a divorce on the grounds of his adultery and cruelty, but he was required to pay her alimony of £300 per annum. But that was the easy part. She then had to try to recover custody of the children, in an age where the law presumed that her husband had sole rights in the matter.

First though, there was the matter of an appeal lodged by her husband at the Court of Arches. Before the case even reached the appeal court Mr Bowes seized his wife, bundled her into a carriage and, having kidnapped her, subjected her to extraordinary hardship as he headed north, probably intending to abduct her to Ireland. He was eventually caught and Mary was set free. She then brought a suit in Chancery aimed at recovering all her assets, but had to do so in the name of her trustee since she herself had no right to sue. Fortuitously, she had settled a large part of her property in the names of trustees before her second marriage, and the question before the courts was whether this was actually lawful, or whether, as her husband claimed, it was an outrageous attempt to deny him what was rightfully his. Mary won a staggering victory, overturning the long held presumption that all property brought into the marriage belonged to the husband. Nearly a century passed before the Married Women's Property Act of 1870 put female property rights onto the statute book. But Mary's litigation was not over. She continued to press for custody of her children, and in 1790 finally persuaded the courts that her husband, by now languishing in prison for unpaid debts, should have no further part in their upbringing. It was a remarkable success – all the more so because the judgment stood almost alone for the next fifty years. It did not open the floodgates to others, largely because the verdicts of enlightened reformers such as Lord Mansfield were followed up by a crackdown lasting half a century under the influence of men like Lord Eldon and Lord Kenyon. This was an age where the law could be made by judges, and under the auspices of these arch-conservatives the pendulum swung back in favour of the rights of husbands. In general, throughout the Georgian era, children were the sole legal responsibility of the father: mothers had no rights at all.

PRIMOGENITURE and ENTAILED INTERESTS

Linked closely with coverture was the custom of primogeniture. It was not enshrined in the law – no statute forbade testators from sharing their estates equally between their children of either gender. But custom and practice developed whereby landowners chose to leave their estates to the eldest son. In order to tie up the estate and prevent it being sold outside the family, a device was used to prevent the beneficiary, i.e. the eldest son, from ever parting with it. This was achieved by creating an interest in land known as a 'fee tail' (from the French *taille*, to cut or limit). The eldest son would be granted a life interest, and on his death the estate passed to his eldest son, and so on. As Adam Smith said in his 1776 book *The Wealth of Nations*:

> *Entails are the natural consequences of the law of primogeniture. They were introduced to preserve a certain lineal succession of which the law of primogeniture first gave the idea, and to hinder any part of the original estate from being carried out of the proposed line either by gift, devise or alienation.*

What was known as the 'Rule against Perpetuities' prevented land being tied up indefinitely, but it was still possible to create a succession of life interests, effectively locking the estate up for a considerable period – for two, and sometimes three, generations. Not only did primogeniture exclude younger sons from inheriting, it was generally used to prevent any part of the main estate (the titles, the land and the income) passing to daughters. You only have to think of the Bennet girls in *Pride and Prejudice* to see the profound effect which an entail could have on the dynamics of family life. Mr Bennet only had a life interest, and having produced five daughters but no sons, his estate would automatically pass to his cousin, the smarmy Mr Collins.

But if the main estate was bequeathed to an eldest son, it followed that some sort of provision had to be made for younger sons, and for daughters. This was usually achieved in the case of younger sons by providing a sum of money – a cash settlement – sufficient to enable the young man to make his way in the world. This might be by the purchase of a commission in the army, or funding the son's education while he trained at the Bar in order to become a barrister, or involve the acquisition of a living for a son aspiring to enter the church. For the girls, there were other legal devices, such as jointures, marriage portions and annuities.

A jointure was often set up at the time of marriage and made provision for an annual income to be paid to the wife in the event of her being widowed. In other words property would be settled on the joint lives of the happy couple, but on the basis that it would pass to the widow on the husband's death. It could be established before or after the marriage. The wife's family might choose to make a payment to the husband. By way of exchange the husband would agree a jointure (usually being more than a third of the sum advanced) and this would be settled on her for her lifetime.

A marriage portion was a lump sum, paid by the bride and brought into the marriage. In the case of Mrs Bennet in *Pride and Prejudice* the sum involved was £5,000 and hence her daughters' portion from her estate would be £1,000 each. An annuity was also often given to avoid hardship on the part of an unmarried female relative. In this way, the real-life Jane Austen received an annuity of £50 a year from her brother, as did her widowed mother. However, all of these legal devices have to be seen in the context that they really only worked to provide money for spinsters and widows. During the actual marriage the income, be it from the annuity, or the portion or jointure, belonged to the husband.

It is interesting to see how the status of marriage is represented in literature. In Daniel Defoe's last novel *Roxana* he tells the story of a married woman with five children who is deserted by her husband and forced to consider 'alternative means' of supporting her family. She does so by becoming her landlord's mistress, and later moves on to the life of a pampered courtesan. It is a story of how necessity moulded her life – but also about how she becomes addicted to the fame and fortune which accompanies her choice of lifestyle, and how she is finally tripped up by her own children. The eponymous heroine has some choice things to say about the married state:

A Wife is treated with Indifference, a Mistress with a strong Passion; a Wife is look'd upon, as but an Upper-Servant. A Mistress is a Sovereign; a Wife must give up all she has; have every reserve she makes for herself, be thought hard of, and be upbraided with her very Pin Money; whereas a mistress makes the Saying true, that what the

Man has is hers, and what she has is her own; the Wife bears a thousand insults and is forced to sit still and bear it, or part and be undone; a mistress insulted, helps herself immediately, and takes another.

'Pin money' originally denoted an allowance made to a woman for dress and other personal expenses by her husband. It was always used to mean a very trifling or insignificant sum of money, but even this was likely to be used as the basis for a rebuke by an ungrateful husband.

The story of Roxana is of course a man's 'take' on female behaviour. This male outlook is shown when Defoe has Roxana accept that her reasoning is wicked:

a Wife lives at home and possesses a man's house, his servants, his equipages and has a right to own his children, and has the return of Duty and Affection. Conversely a mistress sculks about in lodgings and is visited in the dark.

However, the easy pleasures of whoredom are too strong for Roxana, and she reasons:

… the very nature of the Marriage Contract was, in short, nothing but giving up Liberty, Estate, Authority and everything, to the Man, and the Woman was indeed, a meer [sic] Woman ever after, that is to say, a Slave.

Joseph Addison, writing in 1716 in *The Freeholder*, mocks female power when he says:

Ladies are always of great use to the [political] party they espouse, and never fail to win over numbers to it. Lovers, according to Sir William Petty's computation, make at least the third part of sensible men of the British nation; and it has been an uncontroverted maxim in all ages, that though a husband is sometimes a stubborn sort of a creature, a lover is always at the devotion of his mistress. By this means, it lies in the power of every fine woman, to secure at least half a dozen able-bodied men to his Majesty's service.

Mind you, the same article contains this admonition:

Every wife ought to answer for her man. If the husband be engaged in a seditious club, or drinks mysterious healths, or be frugal of his candles on a rejoicing night, let her look to him and keep him out of harm's way; or the world will be apt to say, she has a mind to be a widow before her time. She ought, in such cases, to exert the authority of the

curtain lecture; and if she finds him of a rebellious disposition, to tame him, as they do
birds of prey, by dinning him in the ears all night long.

Ah, the authority of the curtain lecture! It is a phrase rarely used nowadays, to describe
a censorious lecture by a wife to her husband, often while in bed. Four poster beds,
bedecked with curtains, have long since gone….

It has to be said, it was an age of extraordinary hypocrisy, at least to modern eyes.
Men saw women as fickle, or, to quote Alexander Pope:

Women use lovers as they do cards; they play with them a-while, and when they have
got all they can by them, throw them away, call for new ones, and then perhaps lose by
the new all they got by the old ones.

Conversely a married man might consider it perfectly normal for him to take a mistress
or keep company with a courtesan. Writers derided women for their extravagance and
attention to their clothing – as in Swift's splendidly scatological poem 'The Lady's
Dressing Room' which starts with the verse:

Five Hours, (and who can do it less in?)
By haughty Celia spent in Dressing;
The Goddess from her Chamber issues,
Array'd in Lace, Brocades and Tissues…

At least Daniel Defoe recognised that it was a scandal that women were not given a
proper education, writing in *The Education of Women*:

I have often thought of it as one of the most barbarous customs in the world, considering
us as a civilised and a Christian country, that we deny the advantages of learning
to women.

Instead, women were dependent on marrying well, and as Defoe says in *Moll Flanders*:

She is always married too soon, who gets a bad husband, and she is never married too
late, who gets a good one.

In short, the lack of education meant that most women were denied the opportunity to
gain financial independence; they therefore had little choice but to look for a marriage

which would give them some security – but it came at a remarkably high price because the law reduced them to mere servitude. The lack of legal rights probably mattered very little in a good marriage, but it meant the world in a bad one.

Coverture was a law made by men for the benefit of men. It was calculated to keep women subservient: their place was in the home. Men went out to exercise the cut and thrust of making money, while the wife stayed indoors and ran his household, gave birth and raised his children, and cared for all his needs. And as far as men were concerned, that reflected the natural order of things, and the protection given by men towards 'the weaker sex' more than compensated for any loss of opportunity.

MATRIMONIAL LAW – DIVORCE, SEPARATION and CRIMINAL CONVERSATION

The essence of marriage was that it was a contract – a contract whereby the man agreed to give shelter, support, and protection, and whereby the woman accepted a form of unbreakable servitude. Divorce was extremely rare – and expensive – and involved an Act of Parliament. In theory, it was not just the husband who could apply for a divorce, but in the entire period of 200 years leading up to 1857 there were only 324 parliamentary divorce Acts, and of these only four were obtained by women. The first woman to get a divorce was Jane Addison in 1801 on the grounds of her husband's incestuous adultery. The significant point is that female adultery was always sufficient to justify granting a husband a divorce – whereas a woman had to prove that the adultery was 'aggravated' by something extra, such as incest, bigamy, bestiality, or sodomy. In reality she could only apply for a divorce if she could prove not just adultery, but also life-threatening cruelty. It was not until 1857 that Parliament passed the Matrimonial Causes Act granting both parties to a marriage an equal right to seek a divorce, but even then, the need for a woman to prove aggravated cruelty remained in place and this lasted until 1923. It was only in 1969 that divorce on the basis of incompatibility came into force. Only then was it sufficient to show that the marriage had broken down, moving away from the idea of blame.

Instead of divorce a couple might apply for what was, in effect, a judicial separation (known as a *divorce a mensa et thoro* – a divorce from bed and board) granted by the Ecclesiastical Courts. Indeed, this was always a pre-condition of bringing a Divorce Bill before Parliament. The effect of this was that a man or woman wanting to break the fetters of marriage would be involved in very considerable expense – and years and years of paying lawyers to 'wash their dirty linen in public'. A judicial separation had the advantage (to the man) of meaning that if the wife subsequently bore a child it was presumed to be illegitimate. But, a judicial separation was costly and took many months to come through (years, if it was a contested action) and would only ever be granted in cases of cruelty or adultery.

Other possibilities allowed by the law involved a private separation. With this there was a presumption of legitimacy if the wife subsequently had a child. Neither party would have been free to remarry, but it terminated the obligation to live under the same roof. It might also involve the husband agreeing to pay some form of alimony to the wife, although this was normally linked to some form of bond to ensure 'good behaviour' on the part of the woman. Conversely, the man was always free to do as he wished. In the eyes of the law it was the wife's fault if she committed adultery, and also her fault if the husband committed adultery. Men, perhaps unsurprisingly, saw nothing odd in this anomaly. Dr Johnson saw female fidelity as underpinning the whole idea of legitimacy, writing in 1768:

Confusion of progeny constitutes the essence of the crime; and therefore a woman who breaks her marriage vows is much more criminal than a man who does it. A man, to be sure, is criminal in the sight of GOD; but he does not do his wife a very material injury, if he does not insult her; if for instance, from mere wantonness of appetite, he steals privately to her chambermaid. Sir, a wife ought not greatly to resent this. I would not receive home a daughter who had run away from her husband on that account. A wife should study to reclaim her husband by more attention to please him.

On another occasion, commenting on a woman who took a lover after years of suffering and cruelty at the hands of an adulterous husband, Johnson dismissed her with the words: 'the woman's a whore, and there's an end on't'. We may see it as a time of extraordinary double-standards – but men in the eighteenth century did not. Legitimacy was vital to the whole edifice of the aristocracy and monarchy. Kings and princes could openly sire illegitimate progeny, proudly naming them as 'Fitzroy', 'Fitzwilliam', 'Fitz-Clarence', or whatever; they might be awarded titles, but they could never be appointed as an heir. And so it was down through the social order: married women needed to be faithful in order to prevent chaos.

Illegitimacy remained a bar to inheritance for a further two centuries and, even then, neither of the 1926 and 1959 Legitimacy Acts changed the rules for accession to the British throne, or permitted an illegitimate person to succeed to a peerage title.

The imbalance between the rights of men and women was reflected in the law of 'criminal conversation' – known as 'crim. con.'. This was an action brought by a husband for compensation. All that a husband needed to do was to prove adultery – usually in the form of 'witness statements' (i.e. hearsay) from servants and footmen, and then claim damages against the person cuckolding him. In the second half of the eighteenth century some spectacularly lurid 'crim. con.' cases were heard, such as the 1769 case of *Grosvenor v. Cumberland*. This was a case brought by the First Earl Grosvenor against the Duke of Cumberland, brother of King George III. The errant Duke was caught *in flagrante* with Lady Henrietta Grosvenor and the Earl sought damages of £10,000 against the Duke for debauching his wife, and this despite the fact that Earl Grosvenor was himself a known adulterer. Their Lordships at the Court of the King's Bench in Westminster Hall may have been aware of the hypocrisy, but it did not prevent them from granting the damages, as well as costs of another £3,000. However, 'crim. con.' was entirely one-sided, since there was no equivalent remedy available to a wife seeking damages against a woman seducing her husband.

'The Ladies Waldegrave'. For young ladies such as these, needlework, painting flowers, and reading books with a strong moral tone, were suitable pursuits – running a business was not.

Part One

THE ARTS & LITERATURE

Paradigm:
Women have neither the creativity nor flair for The Arts, outside the home.

Chapter 1

Fanny Burney – diarist and novelist

The bare bones of the story of the life of Frances ('Fanny') Burney give little clue to her influence and importance: she was born in 1752 to a music-teacher father and a mother who died when Fanny was 10. Her family joked at her serious-minded behaviour and called her 'the Old Lady'. She was largely self-taught, dabbled in writing, but threw all her stories and jottings on a bonfire when she was 15. In 1778 she published (anonymously) a book called *Evelina* and went on to publish further books entitled *Cecilia* (1782) and *Camilla* (1796). She spent four, largely miserable, years at Court as 'second keeper of the robes' to Queen Charlotte, but had the sense to keep a diary which chronicled a fascinating insight into the minutiae of royal protocol. She mixed with the most glittering circle of creative and intellectual people of the late eighteenth century. She wrote a number of plays which were either never performed or were taken off after a single performance, and married an impoverished French refugee called General d'Arblay, despite opposition from her father. Her last novel, *The Wanderer*, was published in 1814 and was a flop both critically and commercially. She died in 1840.

Why then is she so important? Fanny Burney, whose portrait appears at Plate 1, was a groundbreaking novelist, a witty and observant diarist and, practically unheard of for a woman, a playwright. In all she wrote four novels, eight plays, one biography and twenty volumes of journals and letters. She also paved the way for other female novelists such as Jane Austen and the Brontë sisters. Virginia Woolf was to describe her as 'the mother of English fiction'.

The accolade of 'first female professional writer' is often bestowed on Aphra Behn, who thrived in the Restoration England of the century before Fanny was born. Nowadays Aphra Behn is mostly remembered because of her short novel *Oroonoko*, which examines issues of race, slavery and gender. Her style and content was bawdy, and Georgian ladies were taught to aspire to the complete antithesis of her lifestyle. Aphra Behn moved in the circle which included John Wilmot, second Earl of Rochester, who wrote some of the crudest verses to grace the English language and died of syphilis at the age of 33. Her own books, her poetry and her plays reflect her own scandalous life.

She wrote not so much about love as about sex, whether heterosexual, lesbian, or gay. In doing so it can be argued that she helped set back the cause of other female writers by a hundred years – she was held up as an example of how scandalous it was for a woman to be an author, and how immorality and indecorous thoughts were a direct result of reading mere works of fiction.

It is against this background that Fanny Burney's achievements should be judged. By the time that Fanny was let loose in her father's library as a young girl, it was a world where unrestricted reading was considered bad for young women. This was the high point of the popularity of the female conduct book, most of which laid great emphasis on the need to control wild imaginations for fear of raising fierce passions. Reading was good if it involved religious studies, such as the Bible, or morally suitable titles such as *The Pilgrim's Progress*. The high point of these conduct books came slightly later, with Fordyce's *Sermons*. Fordyce was a Scottish clergyman who published his *Sermons to Young Women* in 1766, when Fanny would have been 14. At the time Fordyce was 46 and although he was to marry five years later, he never had any children. That did not, of course, preclude him from giving advice about female upbringing. He warned women against attempting strenuous exercise and advised them about what was suitable for them to wear: they should look angelic when they were praying to God. His *Sermons* advised women against public service or going into business, and urged them to develop the qualities of 'complacence, yielding-ness, and sweetness'. Small wonder that in Jane Austen's *Pride and Prejudice* she has the wilful Lydia Bennet interrupt the oleaginous Mr Collins when he attempts to read from Fordyce, leading Mr Collins to comment:

> *how little young ladies are interested by books of a serious stamp, though written solely for their benefit. It amazes me, I confess; for certainly, there can be nothing so advantageous to them as instruction.*

Fordyce was particularly vehement in his loathing of novels, writing:

> *there seem to me, very few in the style of a novel that you can read with safety, and yet fewer that you can read with advantage. What shall we say of certain books, which we are assured (for we have not read them) are in their nature so shameful, in their tendency so pestiferous, and contain such rank treason against the royalty of Virtue, such horrible violation of all decorum, that she who can bear to read them must in her soul be a prostitute, let her reputation in life be what it will.*

His tirade goes on:

> *We consider the general run of Novels as utterly unfit for you. Instruction they convey none. They contain scenes of pleasure and passion altogether improper for you to behold, even with the mind's eye.*

There were of course other slightly more progressive works, especially as the eighteenth century progressed. Hester Chapone wrote her *Letters on the Improvement of the Mind* for her 15-year-old niece, and although she advocated reading the Bible she coupled it with the study of history and literature and accepted that botany, geology and astronomy were also beneficial and that book-keeping, and household management were likely to come in handy in adult life.

Erasmus Darwin, grandfather of Charles, had some interesting ideas which he put down on paper in his 1798 *Plan for the Conduct of Female Education in Boarding Schools.* He opened a small school, which included his two daughters as pupils, and taught them geography, history, modern languages, natural history, embroidery, aesthetics, drawing and mythology. He felt that a smattering of 'polite literature' and an introduction to arts and sciences, grammar and arithmetic would not go amiss. He stressed that girls should be brought up with enquiring minds and active bodies: girls should not write or draw or do needlework for long periods as it kept the body in a 'fix'd posture'. He wanted to develop confidence in his young charges, but not make them boastful.

Mary Wollstonecraft, writing in her 1792 *A Vindication of the Rights of Woman*, laid into Fordyce's *Sermons* as being second only to the works of Jean Jacques Rousseau for their misogynistic zeal. In her chapter 'Animadversions on Some of the Writers who have Rendered Women Objects of Pity, Bordering on Contempt' she attacks his emphasis on women being submissive to men and maintains that women's poor education teaches them to be superficial and ignorant, which only makes life more miserable for their future husbands and children. Mary's contribution is looked at in more detail in Chapter 17, but it is indicative of a growing feeling which developed around the education of women in the fifty years after Fanny Burney was born. However, for Fanny's generation, there was no acceptance of the idea that women should have an enquiring mind. She was brought up in an era where she had little formal education, where reading was frowned upon, and where her juvenile scribblings were consigned to the bonfire because her father, and more especially her step-mother, felt that such writings were not 'proper' in a girl. Even years later this underlying feeling that 'one should not admit to being an avid reader' affected Fanny. In one of her diary entries she relates how Samuel Johnson asked if she loved reading. She replied that she did and when asked the reason for the question he commented that: 'I never see [Fanny] with a book in her hand. I have taken notice that she never has been reading whenever I have come into the room.'

Fanny's response is interesting: 'I'm always afraid of being caught reading, lest I should pass for being studious or affected, and therefore instead of making a display of books I always try to hide them.' So saying, Fanny lifted her gloves to reveal that she had hidden beneath them her copy of the good doctor's *Life of Waller*.

As she said: 'I put the book on the table, and opened it with a flourishing air. And then the laugh was on my side, for he could not help making a droll face.'

Especially scandalous was the idea of reading romances. In 1771 Conrad Salomon Walther published his *Manuel de la toilette & de la mode*. In it he maintained that romantic novels encouraged 'the depravity of the reader'. No honest women should read such books: 'There are books that one must not read in order to remain virtuous and out of respect for public opinion, which quite correctly esteems that a young woman should remain ignorant about certain things.'

There was a general feeling that women were incapable of controlling themselves when aroused, and that reading romantic novels would fill them with lustful thoughts and uncontrollable desires – exemplified by Greuze's picture of a young girl swooning, having read *Heloise and Abelard*, shown in Plate 2. But how much more scandalous if the woman was not just reading romantic fiction, but writing it?

At the age of 26 Fanny published *Evelina, or, A Young Lady's Entrance into the World*. Arguably, the 'young lady's entrance in the world' is a feature of not just *Evelina* but of all her subsequent novels – and indeed of all the novels written by Jane Austen. In effect Fanny also pioneered 'the story from the home hearth' – the eighteenth-century version of the 'Aga Saga' – which in turn was replicated by Jane Austen. Others refer to the genre as 'courtship novels' – and whatever it is called, it became a highly popular form of writing. Fanny was a brilliant storyteller, with a skill at creating caricatures. Dr Johnson referred to her as 'My little character-monger'. Fanny takes Evelina, the young lady who is making the entrance, and forces her to encounter a succession of unforeseen difficulties. In coping, the young girl reveals her true character. At that level if nothing else, Fanny led the way for Jane Austen to follow, because the same plot analysis applied. As with most novels circulating at that time, the novel was written in epistolary style, i.e. as a series of letters, each written from the perspective of a different character. Subsequent books ditched using the device of letters and instead involved the use of free indirect speech – a change which was also echoed by Jane Austen twenty-five years later.

Clearly Fanny was awkward about admitting her 'shame' at writing a romantic novel such as *Evelina*. It was not only written anonymously, but in a disguised hand and the manuscript was delivered to a publisher by Fanny's brother without the knowledge or approval of her father. When her authorship became public knowledge she was both mortified and thrilled – but had to put up with much joshing from the likes of Dr Johnson, Sir Joshua Reynolds and Richard Brinsley Sheridan.

Her second novel, *Cecilia – or Memoirs of an Heiress*, was published in 1782. In it, the phrase 'pride and prejudice' appears three times in rapid succession, with the words 'pride' and 'prejudice' in capitals:

> *The whole of this unfortunate business, said Dr Lyster, has been the result of PRIDE and PREJUDICE….. If to PRIDE and PREJUDICE you owe your miseries, so wonderfully is good and evil balanced, that to PRIDE and PREJUDICE you will also owe their termination.*

The phrase was not only borrowed by Jane Austen as a substitute for her original title of 'First Impressions', but the theme developed in *Cecilia* found echoes in *Pride and Prejudice,* where the parties have to overcome their feelings of personal pride and their various prejudices before they can move forward with their relationship. In *Cecilia* a wealthy heiress requires the man she wishes to marry to adopt her family surname. Her intended, Mortimer Delville, is pressured by his father not to drop 'Delville' and the parties have to come to terms with this clash of wills. The themes of 'pride' and 'prejudice' echo throughout the book, as in Jane Austen's novel, although the outcome is different in Fanny's book because Cecilia backs down. Intriguingly Jane Austen specifically refers to *Cecilia* in Northanger Abbey. Both women wrote novels in which female aspirations, class, and feelings of propriety are examined.

Cecilia contains quotes which typify its author's concern about reading:

> *Her next solicitude was to furnish herself with a well-chosen collection of books: and this employment, which to a lover of literature, young and ardent in its pursuit, is perhaps the mind's first luxury, proved a source of entertainment so fertile and delightful that it left her nothing to wish.*

and about prejudice against writers:

> *…let me counsel you to remember that a lady, whether so called from birth or only from fortune, should never degrade herself by being put on a level with writers, and such sort of people.*

Marriage, wealth and power are major concerns with both Fanny Burney and Jane Austen, and it is perhaps not surprising that the latter was a sufficient fan of the former to become a subscriber when Fanny Burney opened a subscription list to cover the cost of publishing her third novel, *Camilla: Or, a Picture of Youth* when it came out in 1796. At the time, Jane Austen was a 21-year-old unpublished writer, and her subscription of one and a half guineas was a significant token of her esteem for Fanny, then at the height of her literary success at the age of 44. Later, Jane Austen referred to *Camilla* in her novel *Sanditon* when she dealt with the prejudices against female authorship ('She took up a Book; it happened to be a volume of *Camilla*'). *Camilla* is a story of frustrated love and impoverishment, of misunderstandings and jealousy, and the first edition quickly sold out, making Fanny a profit of £1,000. She sold the copyright for the same sum, and used the money to buy a house for herself and her new husband, naming it Camilla Cottage.

It is fair to say that by the time she published her fourth novel, in 1814, her style of writing had become artificial, long-winded and obscure. The book, entitled *The Wanderer – or Female Difficulties* was written after Fanny had returned from a ten-year stint living in France. It is set in the immediate aftermath of the French Revolution and concerns a woman who flees the Terror and seeks to find friendship, but without having to reveal her identity. The novel looks at the difficulties faced by women trying to gain financial and social independence at a time when one's status, and that of one's family, was all-important. However, whereas the publishers anticipated a big readership for *The Wanderer*, in practice it was savaged by the critics and shunned by the buying public. In the eighteen years which had passed between the publication of *Camilla* and *The Wanderer*, Fanny's literary style had deteriorated, and she was forced to pass the baton to newer names and more fashionable writers.

Fanny concentrated instead on her great work, a panegyric about the life and achievements of her father Charles. This resulted in the publication in 1832 of the three volume *Memoirs of Doctor Burney*.

By the time Fanny died in Bath in 1840 she had outlived both her husband and her son, and was buried alongside them in the city's Walcot cemetery. She may not have made her mark with her plays, since only one was staged in in her lifetime (*Edwy and Elgiva* in 1795). Despite the fact that it was put on at Drury Lane and had Sarah Siddons and her brother John Philip Kemble in the cast list, it was taken off after just one performance, at the request of Fanny herself. *The Witlings* had been written in 1779 and contained a satirical swipe at the literary pretensions of her contemporaries, in particular other bluestockings, and never saw the light of day after opposition from her father. The majority of Fanny's plays languished for two centuries and were not even published until 1995, but the one thing they have in common is that they deal with the difficulties faced by women in eighteenth-century society. As such they are of interest to modern-day feminists, but as dramatic works they are unlikely to get more than a passing mention.

If Fanny had not written her novels she would still be remembered for her diaries, which provide a fascinating glimpse into the life of a bluestocking, mixing in the same circle as 'the greats' such as Johnson, Boswell, Burke, Reynolds, Garrick and Sheridan. Although later estranged from her, she was part of the salon culture which included Hester Thrale, and which was known as 'the Streatham set'. She was considered one of the 'Blues' – privileged ladies who attended gatherings arranged by Lady Elizabeth Montagu at her home at Hill Street in London. Lady Montagu had started a series of literary breakfasts, but by 1760 these had progressed to evening meetings. Only later would the term 'bluestocking' gain a pejorative meaning in the sense of a dowdy spinsterish woman; at the time the meetings were a forum for women to express their views on topics which had previously been part of an all-male preserve, such as the Arts, Language and Literature. Fanny played her part in these meetings, which in terms of what would now be called 'networking' must have been extremely important. Men were welcome at such meetings, and Fanny's diaries are full of fascinating reminiscences about her contemporaries.

In general, these diaries give a witty, if sanitised, version of Fanny's life and times. Her description of how she underwent a mastectomy without any form of anaesthetic is quite extraordinary. The diaries remain a monumental testament to someone who certainly raised the profile of women writers. Perhaps more than any of the other women featured in these vignettes she not only succeeded in a man's world, breaking paradigms about what was and was not the right thing for women to do, but she actually lived long enough to see others copy her example. She may not have kicked the door down, but she certainly held it open long enough for others to follow.

'Two Girls seated'.

Chapter 2

Anne Damer – sculptor

Nowadays, museums and galleries the world over are proud to own sculptures by Anne Damer, born Anne Conway in 1749, but in her lifetime her works were often dismissed as being of no importance or merit. If they did show any merit, they were assumed to have been made with the assistance of a third party. The writer and art critic Allan Cunningham, writing at the time, treated her as 'a vain enterprising woman, who is constantly failing in all she attempts and as constantly imagining that she has succeeded'. Writing in 1830, he stated that 'her earliest works are smoothest – her latter productions exhibit most character; but neither are entitled to be named with the productions of first rate artists'. What this patronising critic was saying, in modern language, is that she was fine when she confined herself to 'girlie' activities such as working in clay or making wax effigies, but that she really couldn't hack it in a man's world when she moved on to working with 'proper' materials such as bronze and marble.

She was derided for her love of wearing male clothing and for her close personal friendship with the writer Mary Berry – and she offended many by accepting a commission to sculpt the naked figure of the (very obviously male) god Apollo. The issue was that not only was the statue 10ft tall, and designed to be exhibited at the frontage of the Drury Lane Theatre, but that she was brazen enough to imagine that she, a woman, could portray his godly nether regions! Whereas it was in order for male artists to paint nudes of either gender, and to be fully conversant with the female form, it was quite another thing for a woman to demonstrate that she was familiar with male nudity.

Biographical notes on her life, published in 1834, refer to the insinuation that 'the finest touches in her works were not made by her own hand; but sneers and conjectures do not afford us sufficient grounds for coming to such a conclusion'. The same notes go on to say that whereas 'no-one has suggested that her performances are of the highest order she is nevertheless a woman of fortune and fashion who devotes herself voluntarily and enthusiastically to a laborious and difficult art ... she is, among her own sex, at least, almost a prodigy'.

The only child of a Field Marshal (the Honourable Henry Seymour Conway) who was married to a daughter of the Fourth Duke of Argyll, Anne was brought up in an atmosphere of artistic and literary endeavour in the family's home at Henley-on-Thames. Her father was made Secretary of State and was required to travel widely. When she was 5 her parents travelled to Ireland, leaving her in the care of her godfather and *de facto* guardian Horace Walpole. Later on, she spent time in the company of the historian David Hume. Hume was her father's secretary, and apparently dismayed her while they were travelling on the continent by 'giving a shilling to an Italian boy for some paltry plaster images'. She maintained that she could do better – and promptly demonstrated her skill in modelling a head in wax, following it up with one carved out of marble. It was Hume's praise and encouragement which led her to study modelling and marble sculpture under two of the leading artists of the period, Giuseppe Ceracchi and John Bacon. She also, more controversially, studied anatomy under guidance from William Cumberland Cruikshank. Here was a man who had assisted the great William Hunter as an anatomist, someone who combined surgery with an interest in chemistry and who had written a book on anatomy and went on to become a Fellow of the Royal Society. It was, however, considered scandalous that he was willing to pass on his knowledge of anatomy to a female – and that she should then fill her notebooks with anatomical studies.

Any thoughts of a career must have vanished when, as a 19-year-old, she was married off to John Damer, son of Lord Milton. He was six years her senior, a dedicated follower of fashion, and a gambling wastrel who enjoyed the company of some of London's more expensive prostitutes. After seven years the couple split up: his gambling debts were enormous and his father refused to bail him out. He opted to commit suicide while visiting the Bedford Arms in Covent Garden. The German writer Johan von Archenholz describes the man's demise as follows:

The conduct of the Hon Mr Damer, only son to Lord Milton was … extraordinary, and gave rise to a thousand melancholy reflections. Young, handsome, tenderly beloved by his father, nearly adored by the ladies, and with all the honours and dignities of the state within his reach he conceived a sudden disgust to life.

Having repaired to a bagnio he commanded twelve of the most handsome women of the town to be brought to him, and gave orders that they should be supplied with all manner of delicacies. Having afterwards bolted the door he made them undress one another and, when naked, requested them to amuse him with the most voluptuous attitudes. About an hour afterwards he dismissed them, loaded with presents, and then, drawing a pistol from his pocket immediately put an end to his existence. This happened in the year 1776.

John Damer left a suicide note saying simply: 'The people of the house are not to blame for what has happened, which was my own act.' Other versions of his demise refer to a mere four prostitutes, and to the consumption of not one but three helpings of buttered muffins – whatever the truth, John Damer took his life and thereby left his widow to satisfy his creditors. Lord Milton made it abundantly clear that Anne was responsible for the debts and for the shame brought to his family, and he insisted that she sell her jewellery to meet the liabilities. Lord Milton was not always punctual in paying her the annual sum that she was entitled to under her marriage jointure, and she was forced to sacrifice even this income in order to pay the wages of the household servants, some of whom had not been paid for up to fourteen months.

Following her husband's death, Anna set off on a lengthy tour of Europe, taking in Madrid, Rome and Paris. She was a keen classical scholar, with Horace Walpole commenting that 'she writes Latin like Pliny, and is learning Greek'. She also immersed herself in studying sculpture. In doing so she graduated from exhibiting the usual 'female accomplishments', i.e. working in clay and wax, making medallions and so on, to working in marble to the highest standard. Between 1784 and 1818 she exhibited her works at the Royal Academy on no fewer than thirty-two occasions, working in terracotta, bronze and marble.

Undoubtedly she benefited from having the enthusiastic support of the old aesthete and gossip Horace Walpole. As well as being her godfather he was her second cousin, and became a keen collector of her works, When Walpole died in 1797 he appointed her his executrix and left her a life interest in his magnificent residence at Strawberry Hill in Twickenham. He also made her his residuary legatee and provided her with an annuity of £2,000.

Walpole had introduced his protégé to the writer Mary Berry and the two women developed a close personal friendship which both tantalised and scandalised society. It gave rise to the publication of *A Sapphick Epistle from Jack Cavendish to the Honourable and Most Beautiful, Mrs D-* which was published anonymously in 1778 and was followed a year later by James Perry's *Mimosa; Or, The Sensitive Plant.* Both publications were blatantly and crudely homophobic. Hester Thrale described Anne as 'a Sapphist', but it seems that Anne's wealth and status in 'the ton' protected her from the consequences of such criticism. Her lack of inhibition and her delight in attending masques and balls at places such as the Pantheon meant that she was rarely out of the news. She delighted in taking part in amateur dramatic productions put on at the London home of the Duke of Richmond, and counted the actress Sarah Siddons as her friend. She also was believed to have had a romantic affair with the actress Elizabeth Farren. Hester Thrale waspishly noted in her diary (17 June 1790): 'Mrs. Damer, a Lady much suspected for liking her own Sex in a criminal Way, had Miss Farren the fine comic Actress often about her last Year.'

Meanwhile Joseph Farrington, in his diary in 1798, described Mrs Damer thus:

The singularities of Mrs Damer are remarkable — She wears a Mans Hat, and Shoes, — and a Jacket also like a mans — thus she walks ab[ou]t. the fields with a hooking stick … On Miss [Mary] Berry going lately to Cheltenham, the servants described the separation between Her and Mrs Damer as if it had been parting before death.

This suggests that Horace Walpole may have been a tad biased when he wrote about Anne's 'reserve and modesty'. In a letter to the Earl of Strafford he also described her as being 'so eminently a classic genius', and 'so superior an artist'.

As a sculptress she was beginning to find favour with aristocratic and royal patrons. She met Horatio Nelson in 1798 at the home of Sir William Hamilton in Naples, and her marble bust of Lord Nelson, made in1803, is now in London's Guildhall. Her bust of Joseph Banks in bronze is held by the British Museum while her own marble self-portrait is held in the Uffizi Gallery, Florence. She was responsible for two reliefs dating from around 1786–9 and intended for Boydell's Shakespeare Gallery, and also for a statue of George III carved in marble, to be found in the Register House, Edinburgh. In addition, she created representations of the heads of the river gods, Isis and Thamesis, which can still be seen as the keystones on either side of the bridge spanning the River Thames at Henley.

The Treaty of Amiens in 1802 gave Anne the opportunity to travel to Paris with Mary Berry, where they met the Emperor Napoleon. She presented him with a plaster bust that she had made of Horatio Nelson (a slightly surprising choice of subject!) along with one of the politician Charles James Fox, and in return the Emperor presented her with a magnificent diamond-studded snuffbox, which she later passed to the British Museum.

Looking after the gothic pile at Strawberry Hill, with its 47-acre estate, proved too much for her and in 1818 she vacated the 'villa' in favour of Lord Waldegrave, moving instead to the nearby York House. Her new home had the added advantage that it had its own theatre, built by its previous owner Ludwig, Count von Starhemberg.

The move also kept Anne close to her friend Mary Berry. Mary had a home at nearby Little Strawberry Hill, bequeathed to her by Horace Walpole.

Anne, whose portrait appears as Plate 3, retained her interest in sculpting right until the end, finishing a bronze bust of Nelson for the Duke of Clarence just days before her death on 28 May 1828. She was buried alongside her mother in the church at Sundridge in Kent. In accordance with her instructions she was interred with the remains of her favourite dog, whose bones had previously been kept in a box under the bed of its mistress. Also included in her grave were the 'tools of her trade' – her apron and her hammer and chisel. *The Gentleman's Magazine* published her obituary, adding that she was 'as eminent in Sculpture as her contemporaries Maria Cosway and Angelica Kauffman were in Painting'.

As a woman she was unconventional, and in an age where conventions mattered, her behaviour, her occupation, her manner of dressing and her general conduct were all regarded as shocking. As a youngster she was considered beautiful. Her manners were a source of fascination. She was elegant and yet her very success as a sculptress seemed to threaten the Art Establishment. They resented her, and true recognition of her remarkable skills did not really come until many years after her death.

***

Putting Anne's career in context: she was not, of course, the only artist to make the transition from 'amateur' to 'professional'. In painting, there were token successes when two women were included as founder members of the Royal Academy, formed in 1768 under the presidency of Joshua Reynolds. They were Mary Moser and Angelica Kauffman, both fine artists but tokens nonetheless. Arguably, Mary Moser would not have been included but for the fact that her father, the artist George Michael Moser, was also a founder member. She mostly painted flowers, as well as some interesting portraits. As for Angelica Kauffman, she was apparently a favourite of Reynolds, who had a soft spot for her and called her 'Miss Angel'. It is perhaps no coincidence that when the Irish painter Nathaniel Hone painted a particularly scurrilous picture of Reynolds he included a naked representation of Angelica in the corner. Reynolds was incandescent, but left it to Angelica to go and remonstrate with Hone, who begrudgingly painted out the nude figure. She herself was well respected as a portrait painter. Eventually she settled in Rome, where she spent the last twenty-five years of her life.

Even these two female founder members were not permitted to attend life classes, where the naked male form was studied. And yet, without such study, there was no way that women could aspire to paint that most elevated and respected form of art, the 'grand style' of history painting (i.e. large scale compositions with groups of figures depicting historical or mythical situations). The artist needed access to nude figures for such studies, particularly male nudes.

What was left for female artists to draw were flowers and plants. They could also paint animals and do still-life studies. This male bias was not exclusive to Britain, as demonstrated by the fact that in France the influential Academy in Paris admitted 450 members during the century leading up to the French Revolution, and of these only fifteen were women. Most of those were daughters or wives of members, and by 1800 the French Academy had resolved not to admit any women at all. In spite of this, painters such as Elisabeth Vigee-Le Brun in France attained considerable prominence, just as in England Angelica Kauffman made her mark painting portraits, while Maria Cosway specialised in mythological scenes. They were, however, the exceptions which proved the rule.

Other art schools were slightly more encouraging than the Royal Academy – but only slightly. When the Royal College of Art was formed in 1837 (then under the guise of the 'Government School of Design') female members were allowed to attend life classes, separate from the men, where the male figure wore … a suit of armour! In general, it was regarded as unseemly, throughout the Georgian era, for women to be associated with nude male studies. This resulted in the Joseph Zoffany painting, now in the Royal Collection, comprising the group portrait of *The Academicians of the Royal Academy*. It shows the male founders of the Academy assembled in a large studio, crowded around two nude male models. The two female members, Angelica Kauffman and Mary Moser are present, not in person, but as portraits hanging on the wall. Thus was decorum maintained.

The fact remains: not a single female was admitted as a pupil of the Royal Academy for nearly 100 years. The first female pupil, Laura Herford, was one of thirty-eight women who had signed a petition in 1858 asking that women should be permitted to attend life classes. Two years later she was enrolled, allegedly after signing her submission drawings with just her initials – in other words, the authorities had failed to spot her gender. After the two foundation members, there were no other female members of the Royal Academy until Annie Swynnerton was admitted in 1922, and the first female to become a full member was Laura Knight in 1936. The first female professor was not appointed until 2011. So, rather than the Royal Academy being at the forefront of female emancipation by having two female founder members, it would appear that throughout the first 200 years of its existence the Academy has been a bastion of male intolerance and bigotry.

That is not to say that there were no women supporting themselves through their artistic endeavours. Amelia Long, otherwise Lady Farnborough, was respected for her etchings of landscape scenes, but never had to rely on her artistic talents to pay the bills. Clara Wheatley was an artist who was married to the painter Francis Wheatley and when he died, she struggled to support her family of four children by painting miniatures and illustrations for the *Botanical Magazine*. Later she married the Irish actor and artist Alexander Pope, and as Mrs Pope she was known as a painter of flowers and portraits. She also taught painting to Princess Sophia of Gloucester and to various aristocratic families, but never became either rich or famous. Elizabeth Leveson-Gower (Countess of Sutherland) was an accomplished oil painter and a gifted watercolourist specialising in landscapes of the Sutherland coast. Her etchings of views in the Orkney Islands and northeast coast of Scotland were published between 1805 and 1807 and were well received, but again, the Countess was not exactly short of a few bob. She and her husband owned fully two-thirds of the county of Sutherland, and she was notorious for having instigated the clearance of vast areas of land formerly farmed by crofters and tenants, replacing them with large-scale sheep farming. One of her daughters married the Duke of Norfolk, another the Marquess of Westminster, and no one ever considered that the Countess could support herself and her family through her artistic endeavours.

However, there were others who made money from their artistic talents – one being Anna Maria Garthwaite. She had started to design silks and wallpapers in the mid-1720s, when she was in her thirties. Her designs for silk weaving often involved graceful floral motifs, and she made a reasonable living in what was very much a niche market. Another was the Scottish illustrator Elizabeth Blackwell. Finding her husband in a debtors' prison inspired her to apply her skills in illustrating an important book – a herbal which listed many newly discovered plants. *A Curious Herbal* was published between 1737 and 1739 and was immediately acclaimed by apothecaries and physicians, and was commended by the Royal College of Physicians. Another artist, entirely self-taught, was the wax modeller Patricia Wright who came to Britain from America and opened a highly popular venue at Chidsey Court, Pall Mall. Years before Madame Tussaud demonstrated her skills, Mrs Wright amazed the public with her accurate effigies of the rich and famous. Unfortunately, a fire destroyed almost all of her works, and only two figures remain (William Pitt and Lord Howe). Clearly, she was a talented sculptress earning enough to support herself and her son in London between 1772 and 1786 and was described as 'The Promethean Modeller'.

But for the vast majority of artistic women there was no commercial outlet for their talents and acceptance of them as serious artists had to wait another 200 years.

'London cries – the milkmaid' by Paul Sandby.

Chapter 3

Sarah Siddons – actress

Actresses in the Georgian era were often regarded as being whores. It is important to remember that in the eighteenth century the term 'whore' was used, in its primary sense, to mean a woman who fornicated, and not necessarily to describe a woman who provided sex for money. Dr Johnson in his Dictionary defines 'whore' as 'a woman who converses unlawfully with men; a fornicator, an adulteress, a strumpet'. Nowadays we may see the words whore, strumpet and harlot as all indicating a willingness to have sex for money, but in the seventeenth and eighteenth centuries it was perhaps more accurate to see them as terms applying to all sexually promiscuous and independent women. Such independence was regarded as appalling, and a threat to social stability. Female lusts needed to be curbed, not paraded around in public.

In Shakespeare's day, female characters were taken by boys or young men, and the authorities were outraged when a troupe of French performers arrived in London in 1629 and put on a play at Blackfriars with women in the female roles. The audience was deeply shocked and according to a contemporary report, the actresses were 'hissed, hooted, and pippin-pelted from the stage'. Come the puritanism of Cromwell's Commonwealth and all such attempts to allow women on stage came to an end, with the theatres being closed down as beds of licentiousness and immorality. But when Charles II came to the throne the floodgates were opened: not only were the theatres restarted, but by Royal decree women were to play female roles. For good measure Charles II, then did his best to encourage the trend by making at least two of them his mistress – Mary ('Moll') Davis and Eleanor ('Nell') Gwynn. 'Pretty, witty, Nell' (as Pepys described her), had met the king at the Duke's House Theatre in around 1668, and was probably the only one of his innumerable mistresses who loved him. Moll Davis, on the other hand, (whom the wife of Samuel Pepys called 'the most impertinent slut in the world') had retired from the stage in 1668, but in her time had been famous as a singer, a dancer and comedienne – and a whore. They helped establish a tradition of attractive performers treading the boards and making themselves available to paying customers.

It was no coincidence that the new theatres sprang up in the area around Covent Garden where the brothels and bagnios were situated. The whole area became a monument to harlotry – with actresses playing seducers and young lovers on stage, then cavorting with the audience in the taverns and bawdy-houses afterwards. Theatre managers were eager to give employment to girls who would please the most raucous and unruly of audiences, and even a modicum of talent as a singer or dancer was sufficient to get them a job. In turn, playwrights developed the idea of 'breeches parts' – roles specifically designed for women to appear in male guise, wearing breeches. Think of today's 'Principal Boy' in the pantomime and you begin to realise what a sensation it was to see a woman's legs, at a time when conventional dresses were all-concealing.

This then was the background to the life of Sarah Siddons who, as Sarah Kemble, entered the world in a backroom of the Shoulder of Mutton public house in Brecon, in 1755. She was to become the eldest of twelve children born into a remarkably theatrical family. Of her siblings, seven went on to tread the boards (four sisters and three brothers). Her brother, John Philip Kemble, became one of the most famous actors and theatre–managers of his time, being the manager of the Drury Lane theatre from 1788, on and off until 1802. In 1803 he took over as manager of the Covent Garden theatre.

Something of the strength and depth of the remarkable Kemble dynasty is shown in a fascinating painting by George Henry Harlow entitled 'The Court at the Trial of Queen Katherine'. It shows various members of the Kemble family in an 1806 production of Henry VIII – Sarah plays the role of the queen. Her brother John Philip Kemble the scarlet-robed Cardinal Wolsey, while two other brothers play Thomas Cromwell and the King. The influence of the Kemble dynasty was to go on to the next generation, with Sarah's son Henry Kemble becoming an actor along with his cousin (and namesake). But out of this remarkable family, Sarah made the biggest impact and did more than any other actress of the Georgian era to counteract the stigma of women appearing on stage.

Sarah's father, Roger Kemble, had married Sarah Ward in 1753. Sarah Ward had promised her actor–manager father that she would never marry an actor – a promise which her father said she had never broken 'for you have married a man who neither is, nor ever can be, an actor'. In practice, Roger set himself up as the manager of a group of itinerant performers calling themselves the Warwickshire Company of Comedians, and put on plays on a circuit which took in not just Warwickshire and Worcester, but across to Brecon, over to Coventry and the Midlands, and up to York. Roger performed regularly on stage and young Sarah appeared on stage even as an infant, reciting poetry, singing songs and so on. By the age of 12 she was appearing in named roles in touring productions including one at The King's Head Inn at Worcester in February 1767. A young member of the troupe was William Siddons, with whom she fell head over heels in love. He was eleven years her senior, and her parents were not exactly enamoured at the idea of her throwing herself away on a struggling, and largely inexperienced, actor. He was good looking, and he was versatile – both attributes which suggested that he would rarely be unemployed. But the Kembles hoped that their daughter would fall for the charms of a landowner by the name of Mr Evans, who had an income of £300 a year to his name and who appears to have become besotted with Sarah when she was a young teenager. The parents were not at all happy at the thought of her throwing away respectability for the hand of a strolling player whose father ran a public house in Walsall. In vain the Kembles packed the young Sarah off to work as a Lady's Maid for Lady Greatheed at Guy's Cliffe House, in Warwickshire. She lasted nearly two years, but seemed more of a companion than a maid, and persuaded her family to let her come home – and indeed to marry William Siddons. They wed on 26 November 1773 at Holy Trinity Church, Coventry. She was 19, whereas he was just short of his thirtieth birthday.

Initially the couple continued to work for the father's acting group but opted for a measure of independence in 1774 when they joined Chamberlain and Crump's company, setting up for the summer in the fashionable spa town of Cheltenham. Sarah's memoirs written in old age suggest that it was here in Cheltenham that she first became aware of her extraordinary effect on theatregoers. At the time she was appearing as Belvedira in Thomas Otway's *Venice Preserv'd*. Remember, at that time it was not unusual for audiences to fill the play with noisy chatter, with much socialising, and even drinking and gambling during the play. Sarah noted:

> *I heard some very unusual and apparently suppressed noises … I therefore concluded the fashionables were now in the full enjoyment of their anticipated amusement, tittering and laughing as I thought most cruelly and without mercy. The play ended, and I returned home grievously vexed and mortified.*

It was only later the next day that her husband met up with Lord Aylesbury, who explained that the ladies in his party had been so overcome with the strength of Sarah's performance that they had wept uncontrollably. Shortly afterwards Sarah had a visit from Henrietta Boyle, stepdaughter of Thomas Brudenell-Bruce, second Baron of Tottenham. She was much taken with Sarah and as Sarah herself put it: '…that lovely sweet generous creature – then about 18 – encouraged and soothed me…'. Henrietta also lent her clothing to supplement her wardrobe, while her stepfather made a point of mentioning Sarah's name to David Garrick. Garrick was approaching the end of his career as London's foremost actor and theatre manager, but clearly was still interested in promoting new talent. However, Sarah was pregnant and gave birth to her first child, Henry Siddons, in October 1774. Garrick sent out a number of feelers in 1775 about Sarah's availability, gaining favourable reports back from friends and contacts in the profession. One letter to Garrick from his friend Rev Henry Bate ends with the comment: 'N.B. She is the most extraordinary quick study I have ever heard of – this cannot be amiss, for if I recollect right we have a sufficient number of the leaden-headed ones at D. Lane already.'

Drury Lane was not the only theatre keen to encourage fresh blood from the provinces, with interest being shown by the management at Covent Garden. Sarah's timing was none too good – she was pregnant again and gave birth to a second child, Sally, in November 1775. However, she travelled to London the following month and was due to appear on stage immediately after Christmas, playing the part of Portia in *The Merchant of Venice*. London lay at her feet. But then something totally unexpected happened: she bombed. Whether it was stage fright, or lack of stagecraft given that nothing would have prepared her for the huge London stage – far larger than anything she would have come across in the provinces – or whether she was worn out by her pregnancy, the result was a disaster. She was panned by the critics for her vulgar tones and for lacking spirit. She was wooden, she could not project her voice. This was not the coronation she had dreamed about; it was a humiliating disaster. She soldiered on, still learning her craft, but unwittingly caught up in the crossfire between Garrick and his two leading ladies of the time, Mrs Yates and Miss Younge. Basically, she was thrown to the wolves, and they tore her apart. She was given comedy roles for which she was ill-suited. She was given costumes to wear which did nothing for her figure. For six months she soldiered on, fulfilling her contract, and when the London season ended, she headed for Birmingham fully expecting that she would be given a second chance the following year. It was not to be – she was sacked, 'her services no longer required'. Or, as she later put it, she was 'banished from Drury Lane as a worthless candidate for fame and fortune'. It was a devastating blow, and one which goes some way to explaining her subsequent insecurity and financial meanness. She hated being vulnerable, and the only way to combat the feeling was to accumulate enough savings to make her independent of life's vicissitudes.

Sarah, whose portrait appears at Plate 4, buried herself in her work, earning around £3 a week as she lived in cramped conditions in Bath. If she was not appearing in the theatre at Bath she was making the exhausting journey to Bristol to appear at the Theatre Royal. We think of the Bath–Bristol journey taking around half an hour by car or train; for Sarah it meant an additional two or three hours in a coach at either end of a performance on stage, arriving back home way after midnight and having to get up for rehearsals the very next morning. It must have been exhausting for her, especially as she produced three more daughters, in the years 1779 to 1782. There were also trips to put on plays in Birmingham and York, but slowly she fought off ill health and depression and started to wow the audiences with the depth of her portrayals. To an audience used to actresses marching to the front of the stage, flinging out their arms and then declaiming an entire speech at full volume, Sarah was a revelation. She added nuance to the pitch and volume of her voice, she could switch from loud and angry to soft and sobbing in an instant, and audiences were captivated. Georgiana, Duchess of Devonshire, was an avid admirer, along with Hester Thrale and Hannah More. Thomas Sheridan, father of the playwright Richard Brinsley Sheridan, was a big fan of her acting, and slowly she was introduced to a circle of influential friends who helped make Bath that most fashionable of places. Her fame spread, and inevitably this was accompanied by pleas for her to return to the London stage.

October 1782 saw her greatest test. Six years after her previous dreadful experience in London she was tempted to return. At the age of 28, and watched by her father who had travelled up to London, she stepped onto the stage in *Isabella, or the Fatal Manager*. This time there was to be no dismal failure, but a resounding triumph. London adored her, and the success must have been all the sweeter for having come on the back of earlier failures. She wrote of the occasion:

> *On this eventful day my Father arrived to comfort me and to be a witness of my trial. He accompanied me to my Dressing-room at the theatre, there left me, and I, in one of what I call my desperate tranquilities (which usually possess me under terrifick circumstances) completed my dress, to the astonishment of my attendants, without uttering one word, though frequently sighing most profoundly. At length I was called to my fiery trial. I found my venerable Father behind the scenes, little less agitated than myself. The awful consciousness that one is the sole object of attention to that immense space, lined as it were with human intellect from top to bottom, and on all sides round, may perhaps be imagined but cannot be described, and never shall be forgotten – my dear Father too, embracing me from time to time with joyful tears.*

The press were enraptured at her performance, with the *Morning Post* ending its review with the words: 'A late hour prevents us from dwelling on the merits of this accomplished woman who beyond all comparison is the first tragic actress now on the English stage.' The fashionable elite, known as 'the Ton' descended on the theatre to witness this new star, quickly followed by His Majesty King George III, who promptly invited her to visit the family at Buckingham House. Her wages soared from £3 a week and an occasional benefit performance in Bath, to an impressive £50 a week. The money was not hers of course – it belonged to her husband. He, poor man, was unused to handling money, and was equally unused to handling a wife who was suddenly more successful and popular than he could ever aspire to be. While she was reducing audiences to sobbing, fainting wrecks, he was pursuing the delights of the flesh, and ended up giving his wife a dose of the pox.

Of all the parts most associated with Sarah, her role as Lady Macbeth was the one she made her own. Regicide had an especial resonance with eighteenth-century audiences – particularly after the French Revolution and the death of Louis XVI. It was a topic which fascinated and enthralled the public. Until Sarah Siddons, actresses had a real problem with Lady Macbeth, and tended to emphasise her masculinity. Sarah saw her differently – first and foremost she was a devoted wife, someone who would do anything to help advance her husband. Sarah saw Lady Macbeth as a woman willing to use her femininity to get what she wanted, a woman with passion, strength – and vulnerability. Audiences were filled with admiration and terror in equal measure as she exploited pathos, fear and self-doubt. They were mesmerised by the performances, and women flocked to see a great actress at the height of her powers. She played the role of Lady Macbeth on many occasions, right up to her retirement in 1812, and even after that date in readings. The final performance, on stage at the Covent Garden theatre, has gone down as one of the most extraordinary nights in theatre history. On 29 June 1812 she got as far as the sleepwalking scene when the audience refused to allow the play to continue. There was no way that they were going to allow their favourite actress to finish the role by simply dying offstage. After a period of tumultuous applause, the curtains reopened to show Sarah Siddons no longer as Lady Macbeth, but wearing her own clothes. She then proceeded to deliver a highly emotional farewell speech that lasted eight minutes.

With many of her performances, female audiences could relate to an actress playing 'the wronged woman' – they were moved by the display of raw emotion. Perhaps they went to the theatre 'wanting to be moved' – and certainly they seemed to faint at the drop of a hat. Sarah became an icon, worshipped by her adoring audiences.

Stories of her financial parsimony and greed started to circulate. It was suggested that she was unhappy to offer her services for free when a benefit was being given to one of the other actors. The rift between husband and wife became obvious, and increasingly it was a case that as she made more money, so he squandered it. Her fame meant that her portrait was painted by all the leading artists of the day, especially Reynolds, Gainsborough and George Romney. The young Thomas Lawrence fell under her spell. In later years he was to paint her on at least fourteen occasions, and was clearly besotted with Sarah. In time (during the late 1790s) he transferred his affection to her eldest daughter Sally, to the extent of asking (but being refused) parental permission to marry her. He then switched his attentions to the charms of Sally's younger sibling Maria. Maria, spoilt, flirtatious and more physically alluring than her elder sister, infatuated the ever-so-intense Lawrence, but this infatuation waned when Maria became ill, and Thomas resumed his pursuit of the elder sister. It was at this point that fate intervened: Maria died of consumption in 1798 at the age of 19, but not before extracting a promise from Sally that she would never marry Thomas. Sally kept to her word – but she too was to die five years later. In fact Sarah Siddons was to bury five of her seven children during her lifetime. It may also be the case that Thomas Lawrence was more in love with the mother than the daughters; years later he fell head over heels in love with Sarah's niece, Fanny Kemble, a girl who, more than any other, closely resembled Sarah Siddons in her youth. Yes, there were rumours of an affair between Sarah and Thomas, but these were in all likelihood no more than malicious lies. William Siddons, who for some years had been separated from his wife, wrote to the newspapers in November 1804 to say:

> *Having been informed on my recent arrival in town, that the most wicked and injurious slanders have been circulated of late respecting Mrs Siddons, I do hereby offer a Reward of One Thousand Pounds, for the first discovery and conviction of any Person who had been or shall be concerned, directly or indirectly, in the circulation thereof.*

Not that Sarah was above reproach in some of her friendships; in 1802 she travelled to Dublin for the summer season, which lasted from June until the end of August. There she befriended a young actress called Catherine Galindo, who used the stage name of Kitty Gough. Catherine was married to a fencing instructor – whose Christian name is not known – and during the season Sarah appears to have formed a passionate attachment to the ardent young admirer. He was not even half her age. The friendship appears to have lasted four or five years, during which time the Galindos followed Sarah back to London. In 1809 Catherine Galindo published her account of how badly she had been treated by Sarah, in her notorious open 'Letter to Mrs Siddons'. One-sided and biased it may have been, but it certainly conveys an impulsive recklessness on the part of Sarah. If nothing else, it suggests a woman who was desperate to be loved – not anonymously by an adoring faceless public, not vicariously by the besotted Thomas Lawrence, and certainly not by her feckless husband – but by somebody who could make her feel young again.

The first decade of the nineteenth century was indeed a hard one for Sarah. Her father died in March 1808 and in September that year the Covent Garden playhouse caught fire and was totally destroyed, along with all of Sarah's costumes, jewellery and stage mementos. The theatre reopened exactly a year later, but it was a difficult time, with rioting following attempts by the management to impose higher admission charges. For a time Sarah resumed her career, but by now she was considerably overweight and was suffering from rheumatism. She no longer had the pulling power of the previous decade, and her poor health resulted in less-than-convincing performances. After her retirement in 1812 she continued to give readings but gradually, in old age, faded from public sight. She suffered from depression and entered a deep melancholy after her 40-year-old son Henry died in 1815. Thomas Lawrence was to die in January 1830, and Sarah outlived him by less than eighteen months.

She developed an irritating skin condition called acute erysipelas and died on 8 June 1831 in her seventy-sixth year. She was buried in St Mary's Cemetery at Paddington Green, and a crowd of 5,000 people turned out for the funeral, including the combined theatre companies of Drury Lane and Covent Garden. One commentator at the time remarked:

> *Few individuals ever gained from the public such universal and enthusiastic homage as Mrs Siddons. She was not only honoured with the patronage of her monarch on the stage, but was admitted to the private circle of himself and his family. Such was the feeling of George III towards her that, it is said, he one day handed her a blank paper, bearing his signature, as a silent intimation that, if she had any wants, she had only herself to state, and [he would] supply them. Mrs Siddons did not, however, avail herself of the opportunity, but returned the paper, in the state she received it, to the Queen.*

The eulogy went on:

> *'Majestic' is too common-place an epithet to apply to Mrs Siddon's person upon the stage; it was magnificent. She was somewhat em bon point at the close of her dramatic career, which somewhat but only comparatively, detracted from the dignity of her appearance; but, in the meridian of her success, her towering form, fair high forehead, coal black hair and dark bright eyes gave to her aspect, either in sorrow scorn indignation tenderness or joy, an expression that the term 'sublime' conveys but a faint idea of. The stage may yet be trod by many actresses more beautiful than Mrs Siddons; but that we should ever witness her parallel is as remote an expectation as that of the appearance of a second Shakespeare.*

Sarah's success, amounting almost to worship, may tell us as much about the typical, emotionally repressed, females who made up the audience as they do about Sarah. To them, she was the embodiment of the wronged woman. The audiences could relate to the tormented mother, the deceived wife, the heroic figure striving to be heard above the clamour of a male-dominated world. She certainly raised the profile of actresses and made the stage a somewhat less disreputable place than when she started out. The great sadness was that in her personal life she never found an outlet for the passion she could so movingly portray – in retirement she never found a way of replacing the adulation of her triumphant years, and she died lonely and unfulfilled.

****

Sarah was not unique in enjoying popular acclaim and adulation but, in general, female actors, painters and modellers enjoyed a much lower level of reputation than their male counterparts. Throughout the eighteenth century women were generally regarded as 'dabbling' in the Arts: they were often highly competent but generally self-taught, as painters and pastellists. During the Victorian era women in Britain started to make progress, although not as fast as in France. Nevertheless, more art schools opened their doors to women and when the Slade School of Fine Art opened in 1871, it admitted women right from the outset. During the nineteenth century female artists started to be represented by major dealers, and their works became highly collectable and found a place in the major museums and galleries. On the other hand, it can be argued that after Anne Damer no other notable female sculptors emerged until the twentieth century.

As writers, it was well into the Victorian era before women felt comfortable using their own names. Jane Austen may have followed in the footsteps of Fanny Burney, but she never published a single word under her own name during her lifetime and when the critic and editor Mary Ann Evans decided to publish her own novels from the late 1850s onwards she did so under the male pen name of George Eliot – apparently to prevent any prejudice against what might be termed 'silly-headed women writing light-hearted romances'. The Brontë sisters had their first venture into print (a collective effort of poems written by all three girls in 1846) using the pseudonym of 'Bell'. Indeed, *Jane Eyre*, *Wuthering Heights* and *The Tenant of Wildfell Hall* all became bestselling books published under the male names of Currer Bell, Ellis Bell and Acton Bell respectively, before the sisters reluctantly stepped out of the shadows and revealed their true identities. It was in 1850 that Charlotte finally 'outed' herself and her sisters, explaining that:

we did not like to declare ourselves women because – without at that time suspecting that our mode of writing and thinking was not what is called 'feminine' – we had a vague impression that authoresses are liable to be looked on with prejudice.

But in time this prejudice evaporated, and female writers at last felt able proudly to project their identity.

On the stage the association between 'actress' and 'whore' did not disappear overnight just because of the (generally) virtuous Sarah Siddons. It was a link which continued well into the nineteenth century – and indeed very much later, once it transferred to music hall. *Don't put your daughter on the stage, Mrs Worthington* was written and performed by Noel Coward in 1935; in part, it was a reflection of the precarious nature of the job of an actress, but also reflected the fact throughout the nineteenth, and well into the twentieth century, the stage was absolutely the last place a middle-class family would have chosen for a respectable daughter.

Fanny Burney, Anne Damer and Sarah Siddons are linked together because they were three feisty Georgian women, all married at one time or another, who helped light the fuse for women to have an equal opportunity in the world of Art and Literature. However, it was a slow-burning fuse – and one which was very nearly extinguished by prudishness and Victorian ideas as to what was 'seemly' for women.

Sarah Siddons by Auguste Edouart.

Part Two

THE SCIENTIFIC WORLD

Paradigm:
Women have neither the intellect nor education for The Sciences.

Extract from eighteenth century trade card for John Bird, mathematical instrument maker.

Chapter 4

Lady Mary Wortley Montagu – medical advocate

Lady Mary Wortley Montagu, born Lady Mary Pierrepoint, is unusual in that she could just as easily have appeared in the Arts section of this book (as a travel writer and woman of letters) or in the section reserved for Reformers and Educationalists. Instead, she earns her place in the scientific world because, almost single-handedly, she introduced a medical advance into Britain which led ultimately to the eradication of the smallpox virus.

She led a controversial, if not scandalous, life – summed up in her reputed final words: 'It has all been most interesting.' This 'interesting' life began in May 1689 when she was born, the eldest child of Evelyn Pierrepoint, First Duke of Kingston-upon-Hull and his first wife Mary. Her mother went on to have two more girls and a boy before dying in October 1692, leaving the 3-year-old Mary and her baby siblings to be brought up by their grandmother. When her grandmother died, Mary, then aged 9, was left to be educated at her father's home at Thoresby Hall in Nottinghamshire. Thoresby Hall had an impressively extensive library, and on the pretext of passing her time reading harmless novels and romantic literature, she became largely self-educated in a manner which was never intended for her by her absentee father. Escaping the tyranny of a much-despised governess she taught herself Latin, and by her mid-teens had written a number of poems, short novels and a mixed prose and verse romance based on *Voyage to the Isle of Love*, which had been published by Aphra Behn in 1684.

She entered into a lengthy correspondence with her friend Anne Wortley. Anne's replies were generally written on her behalf by her brother Edward Wortley Montagu and when Anne died in 1710, Edward continued the correspondence in his own name. He went on to propose marriage to Mary – a proposal which was considered wholly unacceptable to her father, by then Marquess of Dorchester. He favoured a union between Mary and the heir to an Irish peerage by the name of Clotworthy Skeffington. Mary eloped with Edward, and married him some time in August 1712. She was 23, and quickly realised that her husband was developing into an extremely wealthy young man, with extensive coal-mining interests in Durham and the north east of England.

The accession of George I to the British throne in 1714 led to the family moving from Yorkshire to London, and Mary immediately immersed herself in court life and became the acquaintance of men such as John Gay and Alexander Pope. She amused herself writing satirical comments about court life, which she termed 'court eclogues' but never intended to have published. The following year she was struck down by a particularly virulent strain of smallpox and was not expected to survive. Until that time she was considered beautiful, but the disease ravaged her skin and apparently destroyed her eyebrows. While recovering from her illness she was aghast to find that her satirical 'court eclogues' had got into the hands of a notorious printer of scandal called Edmund Curll. Given that some of the satires were far from complimentary about Princess Caroline, Mary was forced to lie low and must have been delighted when in 1716 her husband was appointed Ambassador to the Ottoman court in Constantinople. She accompanied Edward as they travelled through Europe on a particularly difficult and dangerous journey, crossing battlefields and enduring an extremely cold winter. Her frequent letters to her friends back in England were to form the basis of a later book chronicling her travels, published posthumously as *Letters from Turkey* in 1763. This in turn inspired other female travellers to write up the stories of their exploits from a woman's standpoint, and led to an interest in all things Middle Eastern.

The couple arrived in Constantinople in the spring of 1717 and she quickly immersed herself in the Turkish culture. She was the first visitor able to give a female viewpoint of Turkish court life, because, of course, the male writers of the time had no access to the closed world in which women lived. Men could have no idea of what actually went on in the female bathhouse (although that did not stop them making wild conjectures) just as they had no idea of the customs and fashions of Turkish women. Mary was both fascinated by the world she encountered, and is fascinating in the way that she reported on it.

Her husband's posting was of short duration; by 1719 they had started back for England, enjoying a variant of the Grand European Tour, albeit with young children in tow. They visited Genoa, crossed the Alps, and spent some time in Paris before returning to London so that her husband could pursue his political career. He became a Member of Parliament and spent much time overseeing his estates in the North of England; she spent her time writing poems (many of them highly critical of the role which society expected women to play) and polished and re-polished some of her travel letters, although not intending them for publication.

In 1720 she began a remarkable process to introduce inoculation against smallpox into Britain. In her Turkish travels she had come across a process called variolation (although Lady Mary referred to it as engrafting) whereby healthy patients were deliberately infected with the smallpox virus – taken from a person who had only had a mild reaction – in the hope that the recipient would also suffer only mildly and would then be immune to more serious strains of the disease. It was a topic which intrigued Lady Mary – partly because of her own experience with the disease, and partly because smallpox had claimed the life of her brother in 1713. Indeed, she had ensured that her son Edward, then aged 5, was variolated in 1718 while the family were living in Turkey, with the procedure carried out by the Embassy doctor Charles Maitland.

In one of her letters to Sarah Chiswell, dated 1 April 1717, Lady Mary described the procedure, which she had observed at first hand:

A propos of distempers, I am going to tell you a thing, that will make you wish yourself here. The small-pox, so fatal, and so general amongst us, is here entirely harmless, by the invention of engrafting, which is the term they give it. There is a set of old women, who make it their business to perform the operation, every autumn, in the month of September, when the great heat is abated. People send to one another to know if any of their family has a mind to have the small-pox; they make parties for this purpose, and when they are met (commonly fifteen or sixteen together) the old woman comes with a nut-shell full of the matter of the best sort of small-pox, and asks what vein you please to have opened. She immediately rips open that you offer to her, with a large needle (which gives you no more pain than a common scratch) and puts into the vein as much matter as can lie upon the head of her needle, and after that, binds up the little wound with a hollow bit of shell, and in this manner opens four or five veins.

The same letter explains that young patients are then left to play together for the rest of the day and will remain in perfect health until the eighth day, when they will begin to show symptoms of fever. The youngster must then be kept in bed for two days (very occasionally three) during which time twenty or thirty pockmarks will appear. After another eight days their normal health is restored. The letter continues:

Every year, thousands undergo this operation, and the French Ambassador says pleasantly, that they take the small-pox here by way of diversion, as they take the waters in other countries. There is no example of any one that has died in it, and you may believe I am well satisfied of the safety of this experiment, since I intend to try it on my dear little son. I am patriot enough to take the pains to bring this useful invention into fashion in England, and I should not fail to write to some of our doctors very particularly about it, if I knew any one of them that I thought had virtue enough to destroy such a considerable branch of their revenue, for the good of mankind; but that Distemper is too beneficial to them not to expose to all their Resentment towards the hardy wight [creature] *that should undertake to put an end to it. Perhaps if I live to return I may, however, have courage to war with them. Upon this Occasion, admire the Heroism in the Heart of your Friend, etc.*

After her return to London, Lady Mary insisted that her daughter, then aged 4, should be inoculated in the presence of the court physicians, including Sir Hans Sloane (President of the Royal College of Physicians and a prominent member of the Royal Society, as well as being physician to the king). The variolation was, as before, carried out by Charles Maitland who thereby performed the first professional variolation in Britain. Lady Mary then embarked on a relentless programme to persuade others to follow her example. The problem was that it met with opposition from many in the medical profession – it was after all, essentially foreign. It was based not on established medical knowledge but on folklore – and Islamist folklore at that. To make matters worse, the English doctors (all male, of course) did not take kindly to a woman telling them what they should do. She was absolutely right in believing that doctors would oppose any experiment which might succeed and thereby reduce a profitable sideline, and yes, she showed great courage and determination in pursuing her cause.

When the royal family heard of the variolation – and in particular Caroline, the Princess of Wales – they called for more research to be carried out. This coincided with a particularly severe outbreak of smallpox in the capital, which claimed the lives of thousands of people, young and old. What was termed the Royal Experiment was ordered, and six prisoners in Newgate were offered a full pardon if they agreed to be variolation 'guinea pigs'. The tests were carried out on 9 August 1721 in front of a panel of court physicians and twenty-five members of the Royal Society and College of Physicians. All the prisoners survived, and all were released. One of those taking part conveniently failed to mention that he had already had smallpox and was therefore immune – he was pardoned anyway. Another guinea pig was Elizabeth Harrison, aged 19, and she was persuaded to take part in a follow-up experiment. Locked in a room with a young boy suffering from acute smallpox for three weeks, she remained free of the disease, thanks to the inoculation.

One of those in attendance at the Royal Experiment as an observer was James Keith, who had already lost several children to smallpox, and he immediately had his young son inoculated. Further tests on young children were carried out, involving a handful of orphans from the Parish of St James in Westminster, and once again, the tests resulted in a brief period of fever and a mild rash, but no fatalities. The success was trumpeted in an official court announcement on 10 March 1722:

> *Their Royal Highnesses the Prince and Princess of Wales, being desirous for Confirmation of the Safety and Ease of this practice ... six persons more had the Small-pox inoculated on them ... and the Curious may be further satisfied by the sight of these Persons at Mr Forster's House at Marlborough Court.*

On 17 April 1722 the Princess of Wales volunteered her two daughters for variolation. The girls, Princess Amelia and Princess Caroline, were aged 11 and 9 at the time. The procedure was carried out jointly by Charles Maitland and by the French-born royal surgeon Claude Amyand. Both girls made a full recovery, and this proved to be a hugely influential piece of propaganda, carried out under the full glare of public scrutiny.

Lady Mary, whose portrait appears as Plate 5, carried on spreading the word, offering support, and visiting people in hospital. There were setbacks to her campaign – especially when variolated patients passed the disease on to others, sometimes with fatal results. Many regarded her as an unnatural mother for deliberately harming her children, some took to writing indignant letters, others published scathing pamphlets and vituperative personal attacks on Lady Mary. She countered with an article written under a *nom de plume*, in which she explained the procedure and emphasised the benefits. It was but one part of a print war in which the medical establishment railed against Lady Mary for promoting an encroachment on their territory.

Lady Mary comes across as a divisive character – people either loved or loathed her. In the case of the writer Alexander Pope he started off as an ardent admirer but, once rebuffed by Lady Mary, became her most hostile and vitriolic opponent. When Pope published *The Dunciad* it was brim-full of venom aimed in her direction, and he followed it up with a decade-long tirade of wild accusations and vituperation. It was not an easy time for Lady Mary: her sister became mentally ill and a family feud developed about who should have control of her finances; her son fell out with her amid very public acrimony; and her daughter's choice of husband (Lord Bute) was approved by Mary but opposed by her husband.

And then, in 1736, Lady Mary fell in love. Enter Count Algarotti, a 24-year-old Venetian visiting London. His arrival provoked an outpouring of passionate poems and *lettres d'amour* from Lady Mary. His visit was short, but when he returned to London a couple of years later, en route to Russia, she evinced the idea of running away to join Algarotti in Venice once his Russian trip was complete. She packed her bags, told her husband that she was going abroad for her health, and waited in Venice. She rented a house, was fully accepted into Venetian society, held regular salons, and was a popular visitor. But still she waited. In time, she travelled around Italy, visiting Florence, where she met Horace Walpole. His indictment of her was that she was full of 'impudence, avarice, and absurdity'. She visited Rome and eventually went on to Turin. Here Algarotti was based, on a diplomatic mission linked to trying to establish international alliances ahead of what became the War of Austrian Succession. Their love affair was over by 1741 and when war broke out she headed for a period of solitary, and almost rootless, existence which was to last for many years. She lived for a while in Chambéry before settling in Avignon in 1742. She fell under the control of an Italian bandit by the name of Count Ugolino Palazzi, who agreed to escort her through war-torn Europe as far as Brescia, with a view to her being able to get back to Venice. In practice, she fell ill while staying with the Count's family, and stayed for almost ten years. She was, in effect, a prisoner of the Count, who came from a family notorious for using extortion and imprisonment to extend their wealth and influence. He forced her to pay his debts, plundered her jewels and stole money from her in worthless property ventures.

It took until 1756 for Mary to escape the Count's clutches and head for Venice. She continued to write insightful letters to her daughter, Lady Bute, covering topics such as the role of women, the importance of female education, and other controversial and often philosophical questions.

Her relationship with her son, at best strained and more often catastrophic, worsened when Lady Mary's husband died. He had made a new will, on Lady Mary's suggestion, leaving the bulk of his vast estate to their daughter Lady Bute and her extensive family. When his Lordship died, in 1761, Edward contested the will, prompting his mother to embark once more for England in order to fight the court case on her daughter's behalf. Yet again she endured the hardship of travelling through a Europe riven by conflict, made worse by her own deteriorating health (she was in the final stages of breast cancer). She settled briefly in London but died at her house in Mayfair on 21 August 1762. Her burial took place the next day in the vault of Grosvenor Chapel.

***

Of all her achievements, Lady Mary deserves to be remembered not just for her witty, lively letters, or her poems, or her trenchant views on the rights of women, but for introducing variolation into Britain. Smallpox was a terrible scourge, and had been for thousands of years. A person had a one-in-four chance of catching the disease at some stage or other in his or her lifetime, and once infected, had a one-in-three chance of not surviving – giving a death rate of one-in-twelve for the entire population. The French philosopher Voltaire gave even higher figures for the death rate, suggesting that as many as one-in-five of the population could expect to die of smallpox. The appalling scarring and the high mortality rate made smallpox a most feared and terrifying disease and yet, thanks to the work of Lady Mary, in time a pattern of immunisation developed. Each new case of smallpox, each new bereavement, each new disfigurement, led to more and more people being immunised. One of those was a young boy called Edward Jenner, born just eleven years before Lady Mary died. He endured an oddly Anglicised version of the variolation process; it was felt necessary to render him weak and less able to fight the smallpox reaction. As a young boy he was therefore starved, purged, and bled while being locked in an airless stable with a number of other boys undergoing a similar 'treatment'. There they were kept, isolated, until the disease had completed its dreadful cycle. Young Jenner never forgot the experience and, years later as a country doctor in Berkeley, Gloucestershire, he carried out experiments using cowpox serum as a substitute for smallpox serum, and in doing so invented the much safer and more reliable treatment known as vaccination. Once more, the medical advance was not without its opponents, and this was picked up on by caricaturists such as James Gillray who joined in the fun, as in the etching shown as Plate 5 depicting people growing parts of cows as a result of being injected with 'cow material'.

Edward Jenner described smallpox as 'the most dreadful scourge of the human species'. It was still responsible for killing an estimated 300 million people worldwide in the twentieth century, but a mass-immunisation programme spearheaded by the World Health Organisation led them to declare in 1980 that the disease had been eradicated throughout the entire world. While much of the credit must go to Dr Jenner, his work was based upon the achievements of an indefatigable Lady Mary; without her stubborn determination in spreading the word about variolation, millions more people would have died. And that is not a bad thing to be remembered for – man or woman!

Journal extracts from diarist Richard Hall for 13 October 1784 describing the inoculation of his 2-year-old daughter. It reads 'This day poor little Anna, her cousins Maria and Eliza were inoculated for the smallpox – may the Lord of his great mercy be pleased to carry safely through and spare them.' By 21 October he wrote that 'the smallpox came out in poor Anna & Eliza – may the Lord still mercifully appear and preserve'.

Chapter 5

Jane Marcet – scientific book writer

Jane Marcet was one of twelve children. She was born in England in 1769 to an English mother and a Swiss banker named Anthony Francis Haldiband, and she disproved the adage that women and science didn't mix. Her education reflected Swiss attitudes towards gender equality and education, meaning that she was brought up and educated with her brothers, learning Latin and French and being encouraged to develop a questioning approach to everything. She was curious and she was intelligent. When she was 15 her mother died and she took over the running of the household, being responsible for her siblings and looking after her father. Two years later she accompanied him on a trip to Switzerland and Italy, developing an interest in painting. Her father encouraged her to train with Joshua Reynolds and Thomas Lawrence, and she hosted at dinners attended by prominent intellectuals.

In 1799 the 30-year-old Jane married a Swiss-born physician called Alexander Marcet. His real interest was in physiological chemistry. Despite running a profitable and successful medical practice, he lectured on chemistry, and the household regularly played host to the leading scientists and thinkers of the day. Jane bore Alexander four children, and buried herself in learning the language of science, absorbing knowledge by attending lectures, particularly at the Royal Institution, and developing an interest in physics, mechanics, chemistry and so on. In particular, she was devoted to attending the fashionable scientific lectures of Humphry Davy.

Up until that time there were precious few scientific text books used as teaching aids for schoolchildren, let alone teaching aids aimed at young girls. Science teachers were male, and so were their students, and so it was a complete breakthrough when Jane hit upon the idea of writing a basic science textbook. It featured an imaginary conversation between three characters: a bright intelligent girl called Emily, her flippant companion called Caroline, and an earnest and kindly teacher called Mrs Bryan. Not only was it intended to be read by girls, but it introduced to those girls the idea that the person imparting the scientific knowledge could be female. Jane first wrote *Conversations on Natural Philosophy* in 1805 but did not publish it until 1819. Meanwhile she wrote a companion volume *Conversations on Chemistry, Intended More Especially for the*

Female Sex and published it anonymously in 1805. The preface shows her lack of assertiveness, and her need to justify why the book was being written, with the words:

> *In venturing to offer to the public, and more particularly to the female sex, an Introduction to Chemistry, the author, herself a woman, conceives that some explanation may be required: and she feels it the more necessary to apologize for the present undertaking, as her knowledge of the subject is but recent, and as she can have no real claims to the title of chemist.*

She went on to explain that she felt

> *encouraged by the establishment of those public institutions open to both sexes, for the dissemination of philosophical knowledge, which clearly prove that the general opinion no longer excludes women from an acquaintance with the elements of science; and on the other, she flattered herself, that whilst the impressions made upon her mind, by the wonders of Nature, studied in this new point of view, were still fresh and strong, she might perhaps succeed the better in communicating to others the sentiments she herself experienced.*

She may not have been an original thinker – it appears that much of the underlying science came from borrowing her husband's lecture notes – but the way the subject was expressed was Jane's. By breaking up slabs of information into bite-sized chunks, explaining scientific theories by detailing experiments which the readers could repeat, and by illustrating the text with her own drawings, she made science accessible. She was a forerunner of distance learning – a communicator *par excellence*. The book was an immediate bestseller, going through sixteen editions in Britain and twenty-three in America. Unfortunately, her decision to remain anonymous (until 1832) meant that the American editions were often printed under the names of other people, and she received no royalties for these pirated copies.

A succession of other books followed, particularly *Conversations on Political Economy* in 1816. Other science primers became the Regency equivalents of today's *Science for Dummies*, before her beloved husband died (1822) sending her into deep depression. In time, she moved on to writing children's books, and to the constant revision and updating of her earlier works. These revisions continued right up until her death in 1858 at the age of 89.

Her legacy as a paradigm-breaker was hugely important: she proved that women and science *can* mix, and paved the way for female scientists in the Victorian era.

Her inspirational qualities were not confined to women, as indicated by the remarks of Michael Faraday, the great pioneer in the study of electro-magnetism and electro-chemistry. He had started his days as a trainee bookbinder, and the impressionable and inquisitive teenager worked on some of Jane's books. As he later said:

Mrs. Marcet's 'Conversations on Chemistry' … gave me my foundation in that science. I was a very lively, imaginative person… facts were important to me and saved me… so when I questioned Mrs. Marcet's book by such little experiments as I could find means to perform, and found it true to the facts as I could understand them, I felt that I had got hold of an anchor in chemical knowledge and clung fast to it. Hence my deep veneration for Mrs. Marcet… as one able to convey the truths and principles of those boundless fields of knowledge which concern natural things to the young, untaught, and inquiring mind.

***

The scale of Jane Marcet's achievement can best be seen by looking at the lack of education available to women throughout the eighteenth century. Men had argued throughout the century that 'there was no point' educating young women; a girl's role was to run the household and produce a male heir, and she didn't need to understand Latin or study physics to fulfil either role. Education was expected to serve a purpose, and it was necessary for men, but wholly irrelevant for women. Gradually people argued that education of women was a 'good thing' – because it could make life easier for men. Writers like Daniel Defoe put forward what were fairly radical ideas at the time in his essay entitled *On The Education Of Women* published in 1719. The essay inevitably reflects the attitude of a man living in a man's world, namely that female education was good because it would make a woman more sweet-tempered, a better wife and more agreeable when in company. The text of the essay is set out in full in the appendix.

What did Defoe think women should be taught? Well, he has the answer:

[they] should be taught all sorts of breeding suitable both to their genius and quality. And in particular, Music and Dancing; which it would be cruelty to bar the sex of, because they are their darlings. But besides this, they should be taught languages, as particularly French and Italian … They should, as a particular study, be taught all the graces of speech, and all the necessary air of conversation; which our common education is so defective in, that I need not expose it. They should be brought to read

books, and especially history; and so to read as to make them understand the world, and be able to know and judge of things when they hear of them.

The list is reminiscent of the one used by the snobbish Caroline Bingley in *Pride and Prejudice* where she outlines the skills which are needed by any young lady with pretensions to being considered accomplished:

A woman must have a thorough knowledge of music, singing, drawing, dancing, and the modern languages … and besides all this, she must possess a certain something in her air and manner of walking, the tone of her voice, her address and expressions…

For her part, Jane Austen went away to boarding school for some years, at a cost of £35 per term. She also had the benefit of unrestricted access to her father's library (running to several hundred books). They included Thomas Gisborne's *An Enquiry into the Duties of the Female Sex*, which Jane read in 1805, when it was already in its sixth edition. In a letter to her sister Cassandra dated 30 August 1805, she writes, 'I am glad you recommended "Gisborne", for having begun, I am pleased with it, and I had quite determined not to read it.'

In his book, Gisborne, an Anglican clergyman, stressed subordination to the divinely imposed social hierarchy. His book, a religious conduct manual aimed mainly at 'women placed in the higher or in the middle classes of society', covers a range of topics, including the differences between men and women, female education, the importance of making the right choice of husband, and giving guidance on the upbringing of children. By modern standards Gisborne was a dinosaur, but in his day he represented an opinion shared by Jane Austen, that women should be 'sprightly and vivacious', but at the same time offer comfort and cheer to others. It was important for women to read 'improving books' (such as the works of William Cowper – a favourite of Jane Austen). But even Gisborne could not bring himself to endorse the reading of novels – they were addictive and prone to 'secretly corrupt' the female mind.

Gisbourne was carrying on a tradition of publishing conduct books aimed at young women, explaining the importance of being meek and proper, of knowing your place, of minding your manners. Most of the books stressed the need for modesty in dress and behaviour, and of abstaining from frivolous and promiscuous behaviour. Reading novels was discouraged since it promoted flights of fancy and encouraged immorality – a scene reflected in Plate 2, which shows a young girl suffering from an attack of the vapours after reading the love story of Abelard and Heloise.

One of the most controversial of the conduct books was *Woman not Inferior to Man: or, a Short and Modest Vindication of the Natural Right of the Fair-Sex to a Perfect Equality of Power, Dignity and Esteem with the Men* published in 1739. The author described herself as 'Sophia, a person of Quality'. It includes the following observations:

> [Men would think it odd] *to see a woman at the head of an army giving battle, or at the helm of a country giving laws; pleading causes in quality of counsel; administering justice in a court of judicature; preceded in the street with sword mace and other ensigns of authority, as magistrates; or teaching rhetoric medicine, philosophy and divinity, in quality of university professors.*
>
> *The Men, by thinking us incapable of improving our intellects, have entirely thrown us out of all the advantages of education, and thereby contributed as much as possible to make us the senseless creatures they imagine us. So that, for want of education we are rendered subject to all the follies they dislike in us, and are loaded with their ill-treatment for faults of their own creating in us; and which, we are denied the help necessary to avoid. And what is the consequence of this tyrannic treatment of us? Why it finally reverts on themselves....*
>
> *Weak as the generality reckon us Women, we can regulate our Passions as well as the Men and are no more inclined to vice than to virtue....*

In practice, it has been suggested that the author was Lady Mary Wortley Montagu. A response, *Man not inferior to Women*, also came out in 1739, possibly under the same authorship. This device, trotting out well-established male arguments, enabled 'Sophia' to swat such arguments away with her 1740 riposte *Woman's superior excellence over man.*

Dr Johnson, whose attitude towards women included his notorious comment that a woman preaching was 'like a dog on hind legs; it is not done well, but it is surprising that it is done at all', was not opposed to female education, remarking that: 'No woman is the worse for sense and knowledge.' He welcomed education, accepted that women would benefit from being taught languages, mathematics and so on, but from the perspective of one who believed in a hierarchy, with the man sitting firmly at the top of the pile. He was not in favour of equality of status, merely of equality in education.

The status of women was always hotly debated. In Volume 36 of the *Gentleman's Magazine and Historical Review* for the year 1766 a letter heavy in irony was published, calling for the government of the day to be taken over by women, headed by Lady Northumberland as First Lady of the Treasury and Lady Chudleigh as Chancellor of the Exchequer:

The ear of the public has for some years been daily stunned with loud and violent complaints of male administration; I would therefore humbly propose, if it were but for the sake of variety, that a female administration should for once take its turn, and be allowed a fair and candid trial…

The letter garners a facetious response to the plans for female rule:

my own wife caught the flame and by this time there is not a house in the village without the infection; Petticoat Government is now the word: the women are all determined to bear rule in their respective families and unless your wisdom, Mr Editor can devise some speedy and effectual antidote to this threatening calamity there will not be a husband among us who will dare to say his soul's his own.

It is fair to say that for many men the idea of educating a woman was a waste of time. The fifteenth-century expression, 'where there be geese, there be turds; where there be women, there be words', was still in popular use because women were regarded as hollow sounding boards. Theirs was a prattling world of gossip, and educating them would only give them ideas above their station….

Even female contemporaries felt that education should be given sparingly. *The Ladies Magazine, or Entertaining Companion for the Fair Sex* dated 1780 carried a (no doubt fictional) letter from a male reader:

I must beg leave to point out to you one capital error of which too many women are guilty: I mean their entering upon pursuits in which they cannot possibly make a figure, for want of proper talents and capacities….

The letter goes on to decry the idea of women writing books and poetry, and even worse, plays, with the words:

I wish you would persuade your readers to make their own cloaths, and to mind the linen of their fathers, or their husbands, instead of penning rants for a tragedy, or studying flippant dialogues for a comic drama. Many a poor man, I am afraid, has his meat boiled to rags, and roasted to tatters, because his wife or his daughter is too much engaged in their airy flights on the top of Parnassus…

The (female) editor responds that of course a woman should always attend to her duties first, but that if she has spare time, it is in order for her to try her hand at writing. In her words, 'I have no objection to their taking up their pen, when they have laid down their needle, especially if they can happily … acquire both fame and fortune.'

Later in the century *Thoughts on the education of daughters: with reflections on female conduct, in the more important duties of life* came out in 1787, the first published work of Mary Wollstonecraft (featured later). It was nowhere near as radical as her later books, suggesting that women should be educated in order to be useful wives and mothers. Only through these roles could women contribute effectively to society.

Hannah More joined the debate with her book *Strictures on the Modern System of Female Education* published in 1799. But when it came down to educating the rural poor, Hannah confessed that she merely sought to teach the young, male or female, how to read. That way they could read the Bible and gain spiritual guidance. But it was not necessary to teach them to write – after all, that was no use to them as farm labourers.

The eighteenth century saw increasing numbers of daughters of what would now be regarded as middle-class families, being sent away to boarding schools. These 'Dame schools' were generally run by women, with an emphasis on the basic skills of numeracy and literacy, plus French, embroidery, and dancing. If she was lucky, the girl might get to 'study the globes' – in other words learn geography. History was not always considered important – in *Northanger Abbey* Jane Austen describes the conversation between Henry and Eleanor Tilney and Catherine Moorland as they take a walk to Beechen Cliff:

I wish I were [fond of history]. I read it a little as a duty, but it tells me nothing that does not either vex or weary me. The quarrels of popes and kings, with wars or pestilences, in every page; the men all so good for nothing, and hardly any women at all — it is very tiresome: and yet I often think it odd that it should be so dull, for a great deal of it must be invention. The speeches that are put into the heroes' mouths, their thoughts and designs — the chief of all this must be invention, and invention is what delights me in other books.

For the poor, a proper education was not an option. There were charity schools, and specific groups, such as the Quakers, promoted their own schools for young girls. By and large the women who succeeded were the ones lucky enough to have an elder brother who attended school, or who had a father with a library, or were fortunate enough to be educated at home; many women were self-taught. A century which had seen writers debating about female education was followed by a century in which something was actually done about it. By moving the debate out of the library and into

Plate 1

Fanny Burney, otherwise Frances d'Arblay. See page 2

Plate 2

This is how men regarded the dangers of women reading romantic novels – the women would succumb to lascivious thoughts and swoon with lust… See page 5

Plate 3

The sculptress Anne Damer. See page 10

Plate 4

Sarah Siddons. See page 18

Plate 5

LADY MARY WORTLEY MONTAGU.
From an enamel Miniature by Zinck in the possession of Charles Wortley Esq.

Right: Lady Mary Wortley Montagu in full Ottoman garb. See page 30

Below: *The Cow-pock* by James Gillray, suggesting that vaccination could cause people to grow horns and other animal parts, and showing Dr Jenner about to treat a female patient. See page 36

The COW POCK _ or _ *the Wonderful Effects of the New Inoculation!* _ vide *the Publications of y*. *Anti Vaccine Society*

Plate 6

A Man Mid-Wife after Isaac Cruikshank. See page 51

Coade-stone lion on Westminster Bridge, London. See page 69

Plate 7

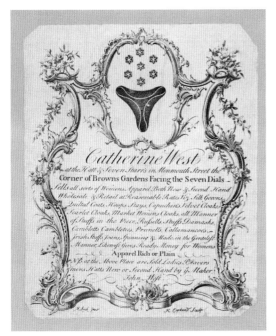

Some women did use their own name in their business: here, the trade card of Catherine West, Jane Batch, Mrs Campbell and Esther Sleepe. See page 64

Plate 8

The Caricature shop featuring the full range of stock characters gathered around the print shop window. See page 78

Two-penny Whist featuring James Gillray, Hannah Humphrey, and their maid Betty. See page 81

the classroom, Jane Marcet deserves her place on the podium. She was not the most original scientist, but she was a most effective communicator.

The century saw one or two more famous scientific figures who were women – such as the astronomer Caroline Herschel. For many years she had operated in the shadow of her brother William (the man who discovered the planet Uranus); she polished the lenses for his telescopes; she shared his night-time vigils; she kept his records and she collated his notes. Finally, she established a name for herself by independently identifying a number of comets, and by correcting the earlier catalogue of all known stars, adding some 500 new ones to the list. She was the first woman scientist ever to be awarded a pension – £50 per annum from the King. She was also, with Mary Sommerville, the first woman to be admitted as an honorary member of the Royal Astronomical Society (1835). Seven years earlier the Society had awarded Caroline Herschel their prestigious Gold Medal. It would be another 168 years before such a medal was again awarded to a woman.

As for Mary Sommerville, she was an extraordinary and largely self-taught woman who went on to write easy-to-read books on astronomy, molecular and microscopic science, algebra and physical geography. She succeeded in a world dominated by men, and shared one thing with both Caroline Herschel and Jane Marcet: not one of them received what can be described as a 'typical' English education. Caroline was born and raised in Germany; Jane had an education based on Swiss values; and Mary was brought up in Scotland where she unofficially sat in on her brother's tutorials. None of them are likely to have succeeded in the world of science if they had been given a standard English education.

Learning to play the piano was not without its distractions. See page 66

Chapter 6

Sarah Guppy – inventor

Sarah Guppy is worthy of attention not because she was a great inventor, or a marvellous engineer, or a proto-feminist, but because her achievements show what could be accomplished when a woman received a reasonable education, had an enquiring mind, came from a supportive family, and where there was enough money to enable her to develop her ideas aimed at improving conditions in the world around her. By no means a feminist, Sarah Guppy proved what women were capable of achieving, but also demonstrated how legal restraints (and, just as importantly, prevailing ideas as to what was 'proper and seemly') held back any recognition.

Born as Sarah Beach in 1770, she was baptised on 5 November that year. Her father, Richard, was a prominent Birmingham businessman, with a finger in many pies including brass founding and sugar refining. Aged 25, she became the wife of Samuel Guppy on 22 February 1795, and went on to have half a dozen children. Her husband was also involved in the metal trade, as a brass and iron founder, and the family moved from Birmingham to Bristol, taking up residence in the highly fashionable area of Queen Square. The family was wealthy and quickly became part of Bristol's fashionable elite.

The Guppys were members of the Presbyterian Church at Lewins Mead in Bristol. Here, members of the congregation were encouraged to support social reform and to consider the lot of their fellow human beings. Sarah had seen at first hand the problems caused by girls being lured into the city from the surrounding villages. She saw the depravity and indifference of female servants and, as an employer, was appalled at the attitude of girls who would show no loyalty and would walk out on a household at the drop of a hat if they could command more money elsewhere, or if they were reprimanded by their employer. It was against this background that Sarah became concerned at the way that servant girls aspired to spend their wages on fancy clothes and ornaments, all of which merely served to bring them into the path of predatory males and into the world of promiscuity and prostitution. Her remedy was to recommend a reduction in the level of wages paid to servant girls – but linked to a strong moral example to be given by the lady heading the household.

To that extent she was no supporter of women's rights, but a product of her time: there were masters and there were servants, and each should know their place. Sarah had published *Instructive and Entertaining Dialogues for Children* in 1800, with the profits going to a local charity school for girls. Other diatribes about female servants followed, and by 1812 she had founded the *Society for the Reward and Encouragement of Virtuous, Faithful, and Industrious Female Servants*.

The family home at Queen Square was also her husband's office and it would appear that Sarah helped her husband in the business. He prospered with his interests in a variety of metal making ventures, particularly linked to the manufacture of nails. In 1804 he took out a patent for a type of copper nail with a flat head for use when sheathing ship hulls with copper sheets, thereby cutting down on the growth of barnacles. It was a development which Samuel Guppy, with support and encouragement from Sarah, sold to the Royal Navy for a handsome profit. Sarah's involvement in the development of the invention of the process, and of its subsequent marketing, may be unclear – some have argued that the whole process was invented by her. What is clear is that it started her off on the path of thinking: 'Why is something done this way, and what can be done to improve it?'

During her lifetime she came up with a number of proposals for improvements, ranging from promoting animal welfare by the re-siting of London's Smithfield Market, to plans for better living conditions for 'distressed female gentlefolk'. She also took out patents for some rather curious domestic products. These included a modified candlestick holder which enabled candles to burn longer, a cooker hood, and an invention which modified a samovar type of tea urn to enable an egg to be boiled in the steam, while at the same time keeping the toast warm on a steam-heated metal plate. In effect it was an ideal breakfast maker. She then came up with an almost 'Wallace and Gromit' type of invention – an exercise bed. This was a sort of bed combined with a gym, with drawers beneath the bed which formed steps for exercise, and with bars suspended from the ceiling for developing upper-body strength. She also came up with new ideas for caulking the hulls of wooden ships in order to make them more seaworthy, and made suggestions for eradicating foot rot in farm animals.

If that was not a varied enough list, in 1811 she applied for a patent, in her husband's name, for a method of 'erecting and constructing bridges and rail-roads without arches or sterlings [buttresses to protect the footings from being damaged] whereby the danger of being washed away by floods is avoided'. Basically, this involved driving deep piles into the riverbank and then using heavy metal chains to support a carriageway suspended above the river. In some ways it seems surprising that the Patent Office felt that this was sufficiently new and different to other schemes to justify a patent.

It was also lacking in any mathematical detail about the strength of the cable or chains needed to make the suspended bridge and with no detail as to how the bridge was to be constructed or how it could be prevented from swaying uncontrollably. It was, however, an important idea, and one which was picked up on by Thomas Telford when he designed the bridge across the Menai Straits to Anglesey, which opened in 1826. He apparently asked Sarah Guppy for a licence to use her ideas, and she readily gave him permission to use them without fee, because the project was for the public good. It does slightly raise the question: why did she want to patent the idea in the first place? However, it also shows her extraordinary philanthropic nature.

It is interesting that when the 2016 edition of the Oxford Dictionary of National Biography came out it contained, for the first time, an entry about Sarah Guppy. The press, with its usual penchant for exaggeration and hyperbole, reacted with headlines which were almost in the vein of 'Sarah Guppy says: Telford and Brunel stole my bridge plans'. The truth is that Brunel was certainly influenced by Sarah Guppy – she gave him encouragement and indeed her 1811 patent preceded his involvement in suspension bridge design. The idea of a bridge across the 700ft wide Avon Gorge, linking the city of Bristol on the east with the Somerset village of Abbots Leigh to the west, had first gained popularity in the preceding half century. A Bristol merchant had left £1,000 in a fund with instructions that when the capital had grown to £10,000 it was to be used to build a toll-free stone bridge across the narrow defile. By 1829, when the fund had reached £8,000, the trustees decided to hold a competition for a bridge design, to be judged by Thomas Telford. It quickly became apparent that cost alone would preclude a stone structure, because the supporting walls would have to be well over 100ft high in order to allow sailing ships to pass underneath at high tide.

All the entries were rejected and Telford submitted his own design, for a suspension bridge costing over £50,000. Despite no funds being in place, in 1830 parliament passed an Act permitting work to be carried out. In the same year the 24-year-old Isambard Kingdom Brunel came up with a plan for a suspension bridge which would cost £10,000 less than the Telford design. The idea of a toll-free structure had been abandoned and in 1831 a second competition to design a new bridge was held; Brunel submitted four designs. One of his designs came second, but before the judges' decision was announced he went to see the trustees and persuaded them that his vision was what Bristol needed: it was not just a bridge, it was a statement about the city's industrial and mercantile greatness. The trustees changed their decision in favour of Brunel.

Sarah became one of the prime movers in seeking to raise subscriptions to pay for the new bridge, which was clearly going to cost far more than the available funds. She is reputed to have helped make models of what the bridge would look like and was prominent in creating an atmosphere whereby the dream could become a reality. She sought no financial gain from the use of her ideas, again maintaining that 'women should not be boastful' about their achievements. Credit for actually designing the structure must go to Brunel, although to be fair it was only built after his death, as a memorial to his engineering brilliance, and then only when his plans had been modified by others; but some of the credit should go to Sarah Guppy for inspiring, cajoling and fundraising. Like Brunel she never lived to see the bridge finished (it opened in 1864, twelve years after her death). She was a friend of Brunel's, and her son worked closely with Brunel, both on the designs for the SS *Great Britain* and the SS *Great Western*. Sarah was also a keen supporter off the Great Western Railway, invested money in the project, and in the 1840s urged the railway company to plant withies and saplings along the railway embankments in order to stabilise the ground conditions.

Her first husband died in 1830, and the next chapter in her story helps to prove how vulnerable women were in the Georgian era. Having been a widow for seven years, Sarah made an unfortunate decision to remarry at the age of 67. She took as her spouse one Richard Eyre-Coote, who was still in his late thirties. For Richard, his wife's money meant a life of profligacy and gambling, particularly on the horses, and before long Sarah was forced to move to 7 Richmond Hill in Clifton, where she remained until her death at the age of 82. By then all her money had gone, squandered by her second husband. A blue plaque at the property is one of the few reminders of her achievements – that, and the large open space immediately opposite the property gifted by her to the people of Bristol, and now used as an ornamental garden and residents' car park.

What we are left with is the story of a woman who did not exactly break the paradigms about women – but she did shift them. In an era of astonishing, world-changing inventions she was accepted by her contemporaries as an inventor and a philanthropist. One suspects that she would have been well satisfied with the article in the *Morning Post* of 29 September 1845, which described her as 'a lady favourably known for her scientific attainments and for the great interest she has taken in Clifton suspension bridge'.

Most of the patents she took out were, of necessity, in the name of one or other of her husbands. None of the inventions appear to have been a commercial success, and to that extent she does not deserve to be up there with Jethro Tull, James Watt, James Hargreaves and George Stephenson. Whereas she may not have been an architect of the Industrial Revolution, she nevertheless helped elevate the status of women, especially in the field of engineering.

*****

No amount of embellishment can disguise the fact that women made barely any impression on the world of science in the eighteenth century. Their lack of education saw to it that they were ill-equipped as research scientists. The following century finally saw a breakthrough, with stars such as Ada Lovelace, the only legitimate child of the poet George, Lord Byron. She was born in 1815 but her success was to come in the Victorian era. She is regarded as a central figure in the history of modern computing and the world's first computer programmer. In a different area, Anna Atkins was an English botanist and photographer, who is considered to be the first person to publish a book illustrated with photographic images. In astronomy, Janet Taylor was one of the very few women working as a scientific instrument maker in London in the nineteenth century. She published works on astronomy and navigation, and ran an academy teaching these subjects. But, as with the Arts, women in Science failed to make their mark until the twentieth century.

In medicine, and midwifery in particular, it is interesting to chart the progress of 'the man midwife' throughout the Georgian period (see Plate 6). Here was a case of women fighting a losing battle; by opposing the idea of men entering their profession they were also opposing the introduction of modern methods of delivering babies – and in particular, the use of forceps. These were seen very much as male innovations, associated with the Chamberlain family of surgeons. In 1671 Jane Sharp, a West Country midwife, had published *The Midwives Book; or, The Whole Art of Midwifery Discovered*, which told women how to manage their births. Four editions had been published by 1725. Her main complaint was against the lack of education given to women, complaining that 'women can attain so rarely to the knowledge of things as many may, who are bred up in universities'.

Later, Sarah Stone became a successful midwife and author of a book called *A Complete Practice of Midwifery*, published in 1737. As an early feminist, Sarah Stone vigorously opposed men trespassing onto her territory. She had only used forceps on three or four occasions and confessed that she found them unhelpful, and that they were no substitute for direct manual intervention. Ultimately she fought a losing battle and, somewhat unfairly, ends up as an almost Luddite-type figure standing in the way of progress.

More surprising was the deception practised by Dr James Barry, born Margaret Ann Bulkley towards the end of the eighteenth century, and educated at Edinburgh University. Having matriculated from medical school she adopted a male persona and name, and as 'James Barry' was commissioned as a hospital assistant with the British Army on 6 July 1813. She concealed her identity thanks to padding, tight bandaging, and an extremely loyal and trustworthy manservant, and ended up achieving the rank of Inspector General, HM Army Hospitals, serving in both the Caribbean and in South Africa, apparently without anyone being any the wiser as to her gender. It can be argued that she therefore preceded Elizabeth Garrett Anderson by over fifty years to become the first qualified female British doctor or surgeon. But she was no paradigm-breaker, no changer of how women were perceived, no shining example for others to follow. She simply succeeded by disguising herself and pretending to be male, even, apparently, to the extent of swearing like a trooper, getting involved in at least one duel over a lady's honour, and somehow or other hiding her condition from the world when she apparently became pregnant. Quite clearly, there were people in authority who knew of the deception, but that did not make her a trailblazer.

Bristol-born Elizabeth Garrett Anderson is recognised as the first female surgeon and physician. In 1862 she was finally admitted to the Society of Apothecaries. This was only possible because the rules of the Society did not prohibit women, but this 'oversight' was quickly put right and the Society changed its rules in 1865 to prevent any other female following in her footsteps. It was not until 1876 that a new Medical Act was passed which enabled applicants to appear on the British Medical Register regardless of their gender.

Part Three

BUSINESS & COMMERCE

Paradigm:
Women have neither the temperament nor acumen for Business.

Making money was a male affair.

Chapter 7

Hester Pinney – lace maker and stockbroker

In 1685 a young man called Azariah Pinney had reason to be grateful as the ship 'Rose Pink' slipped anchor and sailed between the towering cliffs of the Avon Gorge, leading out of the port of Bristol. The vessel, under the command of Captain Wogan, was heading for Charlestown Harbour on the Caribbean island of Nevis. Firstly, he would have been grateful simply to have been alive. Earlier that year he had been found guilty of assisting the Duke of Monmouth in his abortive uprising, and had been sentenced to death for his part in the insurrection. Secondly, he was grateful to a younger sister who had used all her connections, and a small fortune (£65) to 'oil the wheels of justice' and to make sure that the sentence was commuted to transportation to the colonies. Her name was Hester Pinney, and she was to become one of the great enigmas of the Georgian era.

Once in Nevis, Azariah acted as agent for his London-based brother Nathaniel, who was a member of the Royal African Company, and had trading links with the Caribbean. Azariah would order tools and equipment needed on the sugar plantations. He also offered his services to absentee plantation owners, overseeing their estates and managing the plantations for them. Imports flourished and in time, the manifest of the ships making the journey from Bristol to Nevis would include his sister Hester's own contribution to economic prosperity – Honiton lace.

Azariah prospered and started buying property on the island. By the turn of the century he had entered into a partnership with Richard Meriwether, and together they purchased their own sugar plantation called Bawdon's. A second estate, known as Charlot's or Charloes, was bought by the partnership a few years later. Thus were laid the seeds of a slave-based sugar industry which would boom in value in the latter years of the eighteenth century. But this story concentrates not on plantation profits, but on the woman whose unselfish actions and dedication to hard work enabled Azariah to make it past the gallows.

Father to the Pinney clan was a Presbyterian Minister who had been forced to give up preaching in 1662 because of his non-conformist views. Instead, he joined his wife Jane in the business of trading in lace. It was a business which was to involve not just Hester, the youngest daughter, but also her sisters Rebecca and Sarah.

Pinney lace was sold in West Country cities such as Bristol and Bath, as well as in London. The sisters moved up to London to cramped premises at the Seven Stars in the newly rebuilt Exchange Building, but had to store much of their stock elsewhere. From London they could supervise the import of fine quality thread from Antwerp, which they then sent down to Honiton for the lace-makers to use. While in London, Hester started making house calls to promote sales, building up a portfolio of wealthy clients. The fact that she had received only a rudimentary education and could barely write suggests that she must have been a talented negotiator, with a good head for figures.

It soon became apparent that only Hester had the business acumen to make the venture flourish. Both Rebecca and Sarah made disastrous marriages, and almost bankrupted the family business. Indeed, Hester was called back from London to be with the family at its home at Broadwindsor in Dorset, but towards the end of the 1680s she returned to London and by doing so, transformed the family fortunes.

Lace was a fragile, high-value item and it was not easy to wash without damage, yet it required frequent cleaning to remove perspiration marks, make-up smudges, and food spillage. Hester therefore offered a specialist laundry service, charging higher prices than for conventional laundering. She also offered a specialist repair and renovation service.

She was downright parsimonious on her personal spending – she never bought a house, spent nothing on furniture, owned few possessions and spent next-to-nothing on herself. It was said that she changed her address thirty-four times in fifty-eight years, and on each occasion was able to cram all her worldly goods into a single trunk. As often as not she chose lodgings which were regarded as wholly unsuitable by her family – bars, taverns and so on. Family pressure (from her father and brother Nathaniel) generally forced her to look for more salubrious lodgings. She would, therefore, take up temporary residence as a lodger in the home of a professional family, such as an attorney or accountant. Once installed, she could then use her prodigious networking skills to sell lace to the host's wealthy clients. However, it is apparent that she was often pressured by the male members of the family to conform, Nathaniel in particular objected to her leading what might be seen as a 'low life based around taverns' where he writes:

a good name is better than pretiouse oyntment and I must farther tell you that reputacion where God hath accompanied it with tollerable gifts and Beauty hath commanded a greater and better fortune than money It Selfe, although that will not be wanting to you neither.

The business prospered and as a wealthy spinster (albeit one with a reputation for blunt speaking – to the point of rudeness) she naturally came under pressure to marry. She was, however, protected from feeling that 'she ought to marry' by virtue of two things: she could show that by remaining a spinster she could avoid the perils of coverture; and she could point to the way that her sisters had suffered by virtue of marrying badly. Nevertheless, she was under constant pressure, as the youngest daughter, to plan for a future which would involve looking after her ageing parents. Two particular suitors fell by the wayside when she was in her thirties – one, a Mr Hoskins, was rejected by her father because 'all speek Evill of him as a lascivious loose man'. A Mr Cutlove fared no better, perhaps because he had a considerable number of children and dependents in tow.

What Hester accepted, and the family insisted upon, was that her money-making skills should serve the entire Pinney family. She made it, they spent it, and there wasn't room for any other mouths to be fed. When she did fall in love it was with a man who was by far her social superior, one to whom marriage was out of the question. The object of her desire was George Booth, who later became the Earl of Warrington. George was the youngest son of Lord Delamere, and their feelings were mutual. At one stage he wrote to Hester with the words:

> *I can tell you yet that you would have me love you and rem[embe]r our tenders imbraces: pleases me that I can not tell you, the joy and satisfaction, my owne dear heart for so long: would make its clame my heart is thine and only thine and can be happe no longer than my love: finds a return from you.*

George recognised the impossibility of marriage to Hester. Instead, in 1693, he married Lucy Robartes, but he remained in love with Hester and in due course she became his mistress. It was a love affair which spanned four decades. When Lucy died in 1723, Hester's father and brother Nathaniel had already died, and therefore family pressures no longer applied. Hester, by then aged 59, simply moved in with George at his home in Piccadilly, and lived openly with the earl until his death two years later in 1726. Such brazen behaviour took quite some guts in the eighteenth century. Interestingly, their relationship was accepted by George's family. They may not have been quite so happy once they realised that when George inherited an estate from his sister, Lady Vere, which included the Manor of Monken Hadley, he had made a new Will. The document, dated 18 February 1717, made no mention of his wife Lady Lucy. Starting with the words: 'Being in Christian charity with all the world', the Will provided for a number of small bequests. George appointed Hester Pinney to be his sole executrix, and left her the entire residue of his estate. In a codicil, dated 31 March 1726, he released Hester 'from all claims upon her' and confirmed the previous Will, for which probate was granted on 4 July 1726. The estate included not just the Monken Hadley property, but also property in West Ham and Shoreditch, along with the earl's entire portfolio of government stocks and shares.

The bequest was by no means undeserved – because Hester was the one who had actually generated much of the George's wealth. It transpired that from her early days in London she had used the information gleaned from contacts in the coffee-houses to dabble on the nascent stock market. So much for the idea that coffee-houses did not admit women! Clearly they did, although quite possibly Hester would have stood out like a sore thumb. What seems amazing is that other female financial advisers and investors did not follow her lead, and by the Georgian era such establishments had become firmly men-only venues.

The area around the new Exchange where Hester worked was an incredibly tight-knit warren of financial information centres. Apart from the actual Royal Exchange building, a trip down Exchange Alley would have led Hester to both Jonathan's and Garraway's – the main coffee-houses frequented by jobbing brokers, dealers and financiers – and also the Bank of England, East India House, and Royal African House. The Post Office was nearby – all of them contributing to the very latest information and gossip about mercantile matters. Clearly, this was Hester's *métier*.

Hester not only made profits for herself, and for the rest of the Pinney family, but also for George Booth – so much so that in 1717 he appointed her as his secretary. This role, traditionally awarded to a male family member, brought with it considerable prestige, something which Hester used to broaden her client-base by attracting other investors. Her own income soared, to a reputed £1,100 a year. This was a sensational sum, at a time when farm workers in her home village of Bettiscombe in Dorset were getting by on £20 a year. Her investment portfolio included stock in the South Sea Company, an investment which proved catastrophic for so many investors when the crash came in September 1720. Her brother Nathaniel, for instance, lost £20,000 in the crash. Even Sir Isaac Newton, Master of the Royal Mint, suffered a hammering for the same sum. Yet Hester, with her golden touch, pulled out at the last moment and made a considerable profit. Recognising this, Nathaniel wrote to her saying: 'Every Weekes news Paprs [sic] acquaints me with the thousands you have happily added to your Fortune which still increases.' Hester also bought bonds in the Company of Merchants of Great Britain and as trade began to boom during the early Georgian period, so did her personal fortune.

If trading in lace and speculating in stocks and shares were all that she achieved, Hester would not have been unique. She was one of a number of women who succeeded in business in an area associated with fashion. There were others who similarly excelled – as suppliers of millinery and high-end fashion accessories. There were also countless other women who invested their savings in the great stock companies of the day. But Hester went further: she used her connections and the money she had made to set up as a finance broker. It was a time when personal lending came of age, and it was not just the banks and the insurance companies doing the lending, it was individuals. Hester was one of them, and she used her network of connections to establish a moneylending empire. It was common for personal loans of up to £100 to be made on the basis of a promissory note, loans of up to £1,000 on a bond (i.e. under seal) and above that figure by way of mortgage secured on property.

Not all of her loans were without risk and she developed a fierce reputation for giving no quarter when it came to litigation. She was frequently to be found as a litigant, sometimes years after the original loan was taken out. Put simply: you didn't mess with Hester.

In old age Hester was involved in paying for the education of her various nieces and nephews – notwithstanding the fact that Azariah had made his fortune in Nevis and ended up owning two sugar plantations. She passed the property at Monkton Hadley to her brother Azariah and his family in 1737 and continued to look after the family finances until her death on 19 February 1740. She was buried in Monken Hadley church having left most of her estate to her sister Rachel and nephew Azariah in Nevis. It was a personal estate which few ministers' daughters from a rural community in Dorset could have imagined in their wildest dreams. Hester proved one thing above all others: women could make astute financial advisers.

****

Of course, Hester was not the first woman to lend money, or to invest in the developing stock market, but she was particularly successful at it. A distant relative called Martha Gay had shown the way half a century before. Another famous female moneylender from the previous century was the Hereford–based Joyce Jeffries, but it was Hester who took advantage of the opportunities offered by the financial revolution which took place in the 1690s. This saw the creation of the Bank of England and the setting up of a number of joint stock ventures. Life Assurance started to appear (Edmond Halley, he of Halley's Comet fame, published the first annuity tables in 1693). This in turn led to insurance companies advancing money on loan to the cash-poor against their expected inheritances.

Women were by no means absent from taking part in these new investment opportunities – it has been estimated that in the late 1680s, 20 per cent of the bonds issued by the East India Company were owned by women. They also controlled a significant 5 per cent of all bank stock. Nowadays we talk of the 'pink pound' and the 'grey pound' to denote the buying power of particular segments of the population; back in the late Stuart and early Georgian period the 'widow and spinster pound' had a similar impact. Records show that ships – often owned in divisions of thirty-two shares held by up to sixty-four people – were regularly the chosen source of investment for widows and spinsters. Some may have inherited their shares, but many were traded by unmarried women in their own name, especially if they were living in or near ports with a strong seafaring community. Female investment extended to the Hudson Bay Company, to newly operating banks as well as in individual pawnbroker ventures.

Centuries were to pass before female stockbrokers finally made a breakthrough: that bastion of male privilege the London Stock Exchange only lowered its defences and allowed women to cross the trading floor in 1975. One of the reasons given for the delay – 'there aren't suitable toilet facilities in the building' – has been wheeled out on many occasions in other professions and in other situations. It does seem a slightly strange argument for maintaining the *status quo*.

Chapter 8

Hester Bateman – silversmith

Hester Bateman was born the youngest of five children in 1708 and died in 1794; in her long life she achieved considerable fame as a brilliant silversmith. It is no coincidence that all of her achievements occurred after the death of her husband. During the period of her widowhood she took over the family business, guided it in a completely new direction, and established a dynasty of silversmiths which included her sons, her daughter-in-law and a grandson. She was a skilled metalworker, an astute businesswoman, and is often referred to as the 'Queen of Silversmiths'. Her success is all the more remarkable because she was almost entirely self-taught. She could probably neither read nor write, and certainly all existing documents show that she simply made her mark with the sign of a cross, rather than with a signature. She also succeeded as a silversmith despite having no formal apprenticeship; in all likelihood she picked up her skills sitting at a workbench alongside her husband, who was variously described as a chain maker, silver wire puller, goldsmith and silver maker.

She had undergone a clandestine marriage with John Bateman in the Fleet. In all likelihood the union was kept a secret because both of them were in their late teens, and John had no qualifications or apparent ability to support his new wife. Nevertheless, she gave birth to a son, John, in 1730. They subsequently made it 'official' by marrying properly at St Botolph's Church in London's Aldersgate in May 1732.

Daughters Anne and Letitia were born to the couple before they moved to a house in Nixon's Square, Cripplegate. There, Hester gave birth to a fourth child, named Peter, and shortly after that, another, named William. The family then moved to 107 Bunhill Lane, in the Parish of St Luke, Middlesex (just beyond the boundaries of the City of London), where Hester gave birth to another boy, Jonathan.

There are no records of an apprenticeship in John Bateman's name and in all probability he was never a qualified silversmith, working instead from home as a contract supplier of items needed by other silversmiths. Wire pulling involved making wire with a uniform gauge by pulling it through blocks, so that it could then be used to make decorative ornamentation for finished silverware. Watch chain making was another process which would have been farmed out to outworkers like John as a type of cottage industry. Outworking was a method used by traders to cope with the peaks and troughs of business activity, and with the added advantage that the outworkers, operating from private houses, would have escaped the notice of the Livery Companies. The Goldsmith's Company was especially vigilant in policing their industry to make sure that no unqualified tradesman could set up in business within the boundaries of the City, but even their policing methods could not detect what went on in private houses. What is clear is that John Bateman was a skilled craftsman, familiar with working with silver, and may well have also made finished items – such as flatware (i.e. forks and spoons) on a contract basis. These pieces would then be stamped by the silversmith with his own mark.

By 1744 the first-born child, John, had started an apprenticeship as a silversmith, qualifying at the age of 21 in 1751. His younger brother, Peter, had also become apprenticed as a silversmith, in 1755.

Beating silver into shape involved many different stages and skills, some of which involved considerable strength (repeatedly beating sheet metal into shape with a heavy hammer for instance), but also great artistry and delicacy of touch (e.g. beating out the dents made by the original hammering, and burnishing the finished item). It is a fair assumption that Hester (known to all her family as Ester) assisted in some of these stages in production. For this reason, when John made a will shortly before his death in November 1760 he bequeathed all the tools of his trade not to his son John, but to his wife.

On the very same day that John died, Hester went to the probate registry to lodge the sworn probate papers and apply for the grant of probate. This suggests that the death of her husband was anticipated – he died of tuberculosis – and that his widow was extremely level-headed and pragmatic. She needed to ensure business continuity. The probate enabled her to take over John's contracts and carry on without any business interruption, and she traded as 'Hester Bateman and Company' from 107 Bunhill Lane. Hester immediately decided to take the business in a new direction, and to produce finished silverware under her own name. In 1761 she went before the Goldsmith's Company and registered her initials 'HB' as a simple punch mark. For the first seven years she supplied finished silver to other silversmiths rather than accepting direct commissions, and this may have been a reflection of the fact that London was over-supplied with silversmiths and a newcomer making a name for herself would have found it hard going, not least because the marketplace was having to adapt to the newfound Sheffield plate, which was threatening to undercut their cost base. Sheffield plate was a process discovered by Thomas Boulsover in the mid-1740s involving making a 'sandwich' of silver fused around a copper centre. Hester responded to the challenge by producing the silver sheets from which her products were made in even thinner gauges. Less silver meant lower costs.

Hester's punch mark was used by the whole family. The popularity of Bateman silver developed as her designs took her away from the more ornate baroque styles of silverware made popular during the reign of George II, to the simple classical shapes favoured by the likes of Robert Adam, Sheraton and other style-makers of the reign of George III. Her pieces were often adorned with simple beading, or decorated with bright-cut engraving, and the factory output was aimed primarily for use in the home – to adorn the dining rooms and tea tables of the increasingly wealthy middle classes, anxious to display their newfound wealth and their equally newfound good taste.

In time the adjoining premises (numbers 106 and 108 Bunhill Lane) were acquired by the family and subsequently, in 1786, a large workshop was constructed across the backs of all three houses, to create a workshop capable of producing thousands upon thousands of items of silver – everything from flatware to fish forks, from salt dishes to sauce jugs and from tea pots to coffee pots. The next generation of Batemans came into the business, with Jonathan's sons (Jonathan and William) joining in 1784 and 1789.

The matriarchal Hester ruled over the family as its business prospered. She continued at the helm until her retirement at the age of 82 in 1790. At that point she left the running of the business entirely to the family, leaving her home-next-to-the-factory at 107 Bunhill Lane in order to move in with her widowed daughter in Holborn. The business continued to innovate, with Peter Bateman purchasing London's first steam driven metal flattening mill (that is to say, for rolling silver into thin sheets) in 1791.

Hester died in September 1794, having outlived her sons, other than Peter. He went into partnership with his sister-in-law Ann Bateman, using the punch mark of a 'PB' above 'AB'. Ann provided the business acumen and drive which had previously come from Hester, and when Ann's son William inherited the business he was a very wealthy man, passing it in turn to his own son before the Bateman family business finally closed early in the Victorian era.

Obviously much of the credit for the beautiful silver produced under the HB umbrella was due to the skills of her family. It is unclear exactly how much Hester personally contributed to the designs, the manufacture, the marketing and so on, and how much was due to her children. But it was *her* business and she deserves full credit for her acumen, and for her insistence on quality throughout every stage of the manufacturing process. She helped found a dynasty – and one which probably would not have existed but for the fact that widowhood propelled her into the spotlight.

****

Looking at the wider picture, Hester was not unique in being a female silversmith. Others included Rebecca Eames, Louisa Courtauld and Jane Williams. Like Hester, they took over a business which had previously been in the name of their husband. Coverture was no bar to a widow in business, and many were extremely successful, sometimes more so than when they inherited the business. It has been estimated that in the 'long eighteenth century', that is to say including the period up to 1837, there were over sixty female silversmiths registered in London. Many of these were in partnership with men (mostly family members but sometimes with non-relatives) and even, in one case, with two women in partnership together. There are several cases of silver-smithing families choosing a 'theme' to the punch mark used to identify their work. This would then be modified by successive family members, thereby demonstrating that the business had passed to the surviving widow, and then eventually to the son. This was true of the Parr, Lambe and Pantin families, all silversmiths in London during the early Georgian period. Elsewhere in England, there are records of female silversmiths in Newcastle, Hull and Chester.

The question has to be asked: what about other artisan businesses producing goods for the domestic market? What, if anything, was stopping more women from acquiring manufacturing skills? It was not helped by the fact that in London comparatively few of the livery companies allowed women to join. These successors to the medieval guilds had a monopoly on apprenticeships. It has been suggested that only around 1 per cent of apprentices were female. Records are complicated by the fact that a person qualified in one particular trade – say, clock making – might actually be a member of a quite different guild. This might arise if a trader claimed membership through patrimony. An example of this might be where father was a goldsmith; his children (and in some cases that included his daughter) were entitled to become a member of the Goldsmith's Company even though they had gained experience in a quite different trade – perhaps haberdashery. It had reached the stage where, with the Haberdashers Company, less than 10 per cent of the members had anything whatsoever to do with haberdashery. In other words, the vast majority of its members were trading in a line of business which had no connection whatsoever with the organisation which purported to oversee its right to trade, supervising its apprenticeships, granting trade permits etc.

In many such cases the livery company could not be bothered to keep records where a widow simply took over her late husband's freedom to trade. In general, a widow was entitled to carry on supervising any existing apprenticeships. She could not however become an officer, or vote, or have any say in how the livery company was run.

If a man was a member of a livery company, his wife might be in a quite separate line of business – such as millinery – and yet use her husband's membership to enable her to take on apprentices. This was especially significant in the case of milliners, because they had no specifically designated guild. A woman wanting to open a millinery shop within the City boundaries of London might well decide to join her father's or her husband's livery company just to be able to trade. Another company with a minority of 'designated trade members' was the Company of Musicians, whose members really were a mixed bunch. Their records show female members, but that was not to say that they were in any way musical, merely that they had a father who was a member. One example would appear to have been Esther Sleepe, who in all likelihood had trained as a fan maker in her mother's business, but whose father was a musician and a member of the Company of Musicians. She joined the company by virtue of patrimony in 1747. Two years later, in July 1749, she married a struggling young musician called Charles Burney. Her freedom automatically became his, by virtue of their marriage. Burney was to go on to become the famous musicologist (and the father of Fanny Burney mentioned in Chapter 1) and it rather looks as though Fanny chose to play down the fact that her mother was a fan maker, perhaps feeling that it betrayed her working-class origins. Esther Sleepe's trade card is shown in Plate 7.

In some cases women had their own businesses, and traded under their own name, and in others they operated under the name of their husband. One problem in establishing the number of female-run businesses was that records often reflected the legal reality. Men were designated in official records – such as insurance policies, business directories and so on – by reference to their trade, whereas women were recorded by reference to their marital status. So you might get 'John Brown, – haberdasher', but 'J Brown – married'. Nevertheless, it has been estimated from insurance records that roughly 10 per cent of all businesses were run by women, mostly milliners, haberdashers, tailors (especially mantua makers) and peruke makers. The range of shops run by women in London is reflected in the trade signs, many of which are held in the form of bill-heads and trade cards by institutions such as The British Museum and the Lewis Walpole Collection at Yale University. Some appear at Plate 8. They show a whole range of businesses, from mercers, suppliers of hats and cloths to fan makers and silk dyers. William Hogarth even designed the trade card for his sisters Mary and Anne Hogarth, who ran a shop selling frocks – i.e. outer wear.

The actual term used to describe an adult woman could be misleading. A woman termed 'Mrs' was not necessarily married, and it certainly did not mean that there was a husband who set up the business or was 'the power behind the throne'. 'Mrs' was a contraction of the word 'Mistress' just as 'Mr' was a contraction of 'Master'. Both meant the same – describing a person's status, i.e. as a person giving orders to servants. Any woman running a shop was therefore entitled to be called 'mistress' because she would have had staff working for her – and even if she didn't have employees her status meant that she was given the honorary title. It would have been quite inappropriate for her to be called 'Miss', especially as in the case of Hannah Humphrey, who owned the print shop where James Gillray lived as her 'lodger'. For her to be a 'Miss' living with a man would have been outrageous. Calling her 'Mrs' at least implied a 'proper' relationship between the two, in the sense that she was employing Gillray as an engraver. There never was a Mr Humphrey. It therefore follows that women may well have started businesses, and run them most effectively, without ever having been married. Any woman who imparted knowledge, for instance as a teacher, or had a skill such as an artist or illustrator, was entitled to be called 'Mrs'. A few, a very few, deliberately declined the honorific 'Mrs' and insisted on being called 'Miss' (Miss Hannah More being a case in point).

'Miss' was also a contraction of 'Mistress' and originally meant a young girl (but *not* a young woman). Originally, a 'Miss' would automatically become 'Mrs' on reaching adulthood, by virtue of her status or class. In time, 'Miss' became used to signify an adult woman who was unmarried, and therefore from the middle of the eighteenth century 'Miss' started to be seen as being the opposite of 'Mrs'. The honorific 'Mrs' then evolved into meaning a married woman, but it is an important distinction when consulting court records, rent books, directories and livery company records.

A similar honorific title, 'Mr', was given to a senior servant who was in a position to give orders to others. A butler would be Mr Butler, whereas the footman might be 'John'. A man in business, for instance running a shop, was always 'Mister', just as his female counterpart was always 'Mistress'. The modern connotation of 'mistress' as a whore is nothing new, and is simply an example of the considerable number of female epithets used in a derogatory way. 'Moll' and 'Madam' are examples. 'Hussy' – as an abbreviation of 'housewife' – is another.

It is interesting to look at J. C. Walker's book entitled *Hints for a System of Education for a Female Orphan House* published in 1793, because it reviews the trades available to women (or rather, those trades considered appropriate to the author as suitable outlets for female skills). On stay-making he remarks:

> *Within my memory, the Art of Stay-making has been wrested from women and given to men. Now I can conceive nothing more indecent than the permitting the touch and*

eye of a rude artisan, to usurp the sacred rights of an husband. But I am afraid to enlarge on the subject lest I should forget that I am addressing myself to a Lady.

He felt that 'young ladies ought to be instructed in the elegant accomplishments such as Drawing, Dancing and Music', but only by a 'professor of their own sex' because 'we learn from experience, the danger which attends allowing a dancing master to press the soft hand of his scholar in the mazes of a minuet, or a music master to languish and sigh over his pupil at the harpsichord'. Basketware, embroidery and lacemaking were recommended, as was the ability to 'use the Chissel, or turn the lathe' like the Hon. Mrs Damer, or copy 'Mrs Wright's power over Wax', which he thought was 'almost Promethian'. More of Anne Damer, and of Patricia Wright, appears in Chapter 2. Books such as *Hints for a System of Education* possibly tell us rather more about male attitudes towards female education than they do about women in the real world, but it emphasises that job opportunities for entrepreneurial women were limited, but not non-existent.

Another book aimed at instructing parents on 'careers advice' for their children was *The London Tradesman: Being a Compendious View of All the Trades* by 'R Campbell Esq.' published in 1747. It is unashamedly male-orientated, but offers a fascinating picture of the sheer variety of trades and business opportunities open to trainees at the start of their career; everything from the professions to glass grinders, and from 'Jack-smiths' (who made rotisserie equipment) to 'hot-pressers'. The latter needed 'strength and a sound constitution' – one of many manual trades where women were considered too weak to fulfil the criteria. In practice a hot-presser ironed woollen fabrics – not something we would nowadays see as requiring strength or stamina, but a reminder that before the Industrial Revolution many manual trades were very tough. Machinery was heavy and the work highly repetitive. As for females, Mr Campbell suggested that they steer clear of hat-making:

[Milliners] *can have vast profits on every Article they deal in; yet give poor mean Wages to every Person they employ under them. Though a young Woman can work neatly in all manner of Needle-Work yet she cannot earn more than five or six shillings a week, out of which she has to find herself in Board and Lodging. Therefore out of Regard to the Fair Sex, I must caution Parents, not to bind their daughters to this business.*

So what were the trades a young lady could aspire to, especially if she could not get a formal apprenticeship? Mr Campbell suggests she becomes a 'tire maker' (ringlets and curls), a stay maker, a velvet-cap maker ('nine to twelve shillings a week') or a fan maker ('fifteen shillings to one guinea a week'). He informs us that hooped petticoats 'are chiefly made by Women: they must not be polluted by the unhallowed Hands of a rude Male. These Women make a tolerable living by it'.

In practice, an unmarried woman without children could try for domestic service, or work as a street-vendor, or, like thousands of her sisters, dabble in the sex trade. Manual work, including working in factories was available, although usually at rates of pay one third of those available to men. Mothers living in cities might opt for piecework in the home, as was the case with workers in London's East End when William Addis hit upon the idea of making toothbrushes. Rather than have a single factory, with all of its attendant overheads, he pioneered the use of female outworkers, operating from their own homes, to thread the bristles through the pre-drilled pieces of ox-bones. The pay was derisory, and of course unless the requisite standards of quality were met, payment would be withheld. But perhaps the main business for the self-employed woman was running her home as a lodging house, charging lodgers for rooming with the family, often in cramped and overcrowded conditions.

By and large, employment for women was seen as an extension of her household responsibilities, such as domestic service; the needle trades such as embroidery, tailoring or mantua making; plus teaching and nursing. All these areas had low status, low pay, and were often regarded as unskilled. Of course, there were businesses where women of a more artistic bent could make a reasonable living. Some became book illustrators, such as the renowned Elizabeth Blackwell. Female artists painted designs on the new porcelain which swept into vogue, and they made their mark in the world of selling prints and developing the concept of print shops. In a similar vein, Caroline Watson, who was born in the 1760s and lived until 1814, can be seen as the first professional woman engraver, specialising in stipple techniques needed for plates in the booming business of illustrated books.

Other women used their talents in more 'colourful' ways – Charlotte Hayes was a very successful brothel-keeper, who realised that men would far rather pay a lot of money for sex in the comfortable surroundings of a high-class seraglio than pay for a 'threepenny stand-up' in a shop doorway. She excelled in promoting high-end 'nunneries' in King's Place, St James's, and made a fortune. Of questionable morality, and certainly illegal, a number of aristocratic ladies ran gaming clubs, often playing faro with crooked card decks. For years the likes of Mrs Albinia Hobart (later Lady Buckinghamshire), Lady Sarah Archer, Mrs Sturt, Mrs Concannon, and Lady Elizabeth Luttrell got away with being associated with clubs where young bucks, fresh up to Town from the country, would be fleeced of their inheritances until well into the early hours of the morning….

'Modern Hospitality' showing Lady Archer making money – by cheating at cards.

Chapter 9

Eleanor Coade – manufacturer of artificial stone

The Gentleman's Magazine for 1821 (Part II) has this entry in its Obituaries section:

18 November 1821: At Camberwell, in her 89th year, Mrs Eleanor Coade, sole inventor and proprietor of an art which deserves considerable notice. In 1769, a burnt artificial stone manufactory was erected by Mrs Coade, at King's Arms Stairs, Narrow Walk, Lambeth. This manufactory has been carried on from that time, to the present, on a very extensive scale, being calculated to answer every purpose of stone carving; having a property, peculiar to itself, of resisting the frost, and consequently of retaining that sharpness in which it excels over every kind of stone sculpture, and equals even marble itself. It extends to every kind of architectural ornaments, in which it becomes much below the price of stone, and in many cases cheaper than wood.

Apart from the fact that the obituary reads more like an advertisement for the artificial stone products which bore her name, the notice tells us very little about the woman who had just died, the remarkable Eleanor Coade. Her success in business was so great, and so well known, that it makes it all the more extraordinary that few other women stepped up to the plate to say 'If she can do it, so can I'. If ever there was a woman who was in the right place at the right time, it was Eleanor Coade, and because she never married the credit for her success can go straight to her, rather than being deflected onto a husband.

Her start in life was not particularly auspicious. She was born in Exeter in June 1733, and was one of two daughters. Her father, George Coade, was a wool merchant and her mother (also Eleanor) was herself the daughter of a wool merchant. The household was non-conformist, and Eleanor remained a devout Baptist throughout her life. In around 1760 Eleanor left the West Country and settled in London, one of many drawn to the capital with tales of streets paved with gold. She started in business as a linen draper, and must have been reasonably successful. However, her father went bankrupt in 1769 (for the second time) and she was left to provide a household for her younger sister and for her widowed mother.

In 1769 she decided to buy the business of an artificial stone manufacturer called Daniel Pincot, keeping him on as an associate. How she raised the £1,200 price is not clear, but for that she bought a relatively untried manufacturing process – one of many formed in the first part of the eighteenth century looking for 'the holy grail' of an artificial stone which was cheap to produce, could be moulded as well as carved, and which would withstand frost, rain and urban pollution. Above all, architects were desperate for a material which could be used to manufacture architectural details on a mass-produced basis. Up until then, if a client wanted his house to have a portico, complete with twenty ionic columns topped with twin scrolls, the stonemason would have to carve each one individually. Equally, if the wealthy successor to a fine country estate wanted to emulate the ideas of William Kent by populating the garden with carved nymphs, adaptations of ancient statuary, and fancy fountains, he would be faced with enormous expense and huge time delays as each piece was made to order. The problem became even more acute as the baroque style in architecture gave way to neo-classicism: no house could be complete without windows, porches, doorways and even chimneys all carved to the new and often delicate designs.

Many before had tried manufacturing an artificial stone and all had failed. Pincot may have come up with the right idea at his premises in Narrow Wall, Lambeth – but if so, he didn't know how to market it or make it a business success. Equally there is some evidence that Eleanor was a keen clay modeller and may have experimented with her own mixes. Certainly, she exhibited some of her clay models at the Society of Artists between 1773 and 1780, and at the very least was comfortable working in that medium. What is certain is that in the space of a very short time Eleanor was announcing that she had come up with a totally new invention, one which she called 'lithodipyra' – a made-up Greek word meaning 'twice fired stone'. She renamed the factory business 'The Lithodipyra Terra-Cotta or Artificial Stone Manufactory' and set to work transforming the building industry.

Pincot then made himself unpopular with Eleanor by holding himself out as being the owner, and behaving as if he had a proprietorial interest in the business. He did not, and in 1771 Eleanor sacked him for his impudence. In his place she appointed the designer John Bacon (the same man who featured in the story of Anne Damer, mentioned in Chapter 2) and he designed products for the company right up until his death some twenty-seven years later. Eleanor personally hired and fired staff, kept the books and directed operations. Initially she may have been assisted by her younger sister Elizabeth, but she died a couple of years after the factory opened, and Eleanor remained in sole control.

Soon Eleanor was working for all the major architects of the day, in particular Robert Adam, but also for such other luminaries as Sir William Chambers, John Nash and John Soane. They could not get enough of her products. They were relatively cheap; they could be mass-produced off-site; they could be made hollow so that they were light, and, most importantly, so that they could take channels for water pipes. It made the stoneware ideal for taking water off roofs, as well as for fountains where the plumbing arrangements were simple to attach. Because it was artificial, it did not attract the high level of tax imposed on real stone. Best of all it could be worked like the finest limestone, be made to resemble either wood or marble, and would last and last and last. In many cases it has lasted so well that the statues are still as sharply carved today as when they were moulded and carved two centuries ago, as witnessed by many of the stone features at Buckingham Palace, the Royal Pavilion at Brighton, and the stonework at countless stately homes both in Britain and in Europe. There are even records of Coade stone being exported to the United States, Canada and the West Indies, while it went as far afield as St Petersburg when the Scottish architect Charles Cameron used it in refurbishing the palace at Tsarkoe Selo on the orders of the Empress Catherine I.

John Bacon became works manager, freeing up Eleanor to spend more time on administration and on developing sales. This was an area where she showed real flair and ingenuity. Some of the figures made by Eleanor's factory were monumental in size – such as the statue of Lord Hill in Shrewsbury which is a towering 17ft tall, and sits atop a Doric column over 133ft high. It dwarfs the somewhat later Nelson's Column in Trafalgar Square by some 15ft.

In all over 650 items in Coade stone have been identified; thousands more exist but have not had occasion to be tested or repaired. The sheer range of items churned out by the Coade factory is astonishing – everything from tiny ornaments to the Gothic screen at St George's Chapel in Windsor, and from chimneys to gargoyles, window keystones to friezes, fireplaces to coats of arms. Caryatids copied from the frieze at the Acropolis could be made by the dozen. If a man wanted a giant pineapple to adorn his roof, or a pair of figures to sit atop his gateposts, Eleanor was the person to turn to. Some were designed for exterior use, but increasingly the Coade stone products dominated the interiors of new homes. They were all identified in a catalogue brought out in 1784, running to nearly 750 designs. From Eleanor's point of view, the great thing was that the moulds could be used over and over again, making the process increasingly cost-effective. If a tree were to fall on a statue and crush it, the chances were that the mould would still exist and even after fifty years an identical statue could be reproduced.

Following the death of John Bacon in 1799 the 66-year-old Eleanor decided to take a relative into partnership, her cousin John Sealy. He had been working as a modeller for the business since 1792 and like Eleanor, was a pious Dissenter. The business became known as 'Coade and Sealy', until the cousin died in 1813 whereupon it reverted to the name of 'Coade'.

Sealy should get some of the credit for recognising that getting the great and the good to traipse out to humble manufacturing premises south of the River Thames at Narrow Wall was never a great idea, and that a proper exhibition site was needed in a more salubrious area. The eastern end of Westminster Bridge was chosen for the new showroom, known as Coade's Gallery, and here the exhibits were displayed to match the order in which they were set out in a new version of the catalogue. Clients and their architects could reach the showroom over Westminster Bridge, i.e. without having to be rowed across the river to the steps at Narrow Wall. They could wander around, catalogue in hand, and order whatever quantities of pediments, porticoes, statuary and so on that they wanted.

When Sealy died, Eleanor was 80 years old. She appointed a distant relative by marriage, William Croggon, as works manager. He was a second cousin once removed and, like all Eleanor's associates, shared her religious beliefs. The business continued to expand, particularly once George IV agreed to use Coade stone in the refurbishment and extension of Buckingham Palace. When Eleanor died in 1821 the business was sold to Croggon. By all accounts he had hoped to have been bequeathed the business, but he hid his disappointment and bought it from the estate for £4,000, and ran it for a further twenty years. Eleanor, meanwhile, was buried in the Dissenters Burial Ground at Bunhill Fields. Many other Baptists were also buried here, such as John Bunyan, as well as Dissenters such as Daniel Defoe and (later) William Blake.

Eleanor left much of her money to various charities, and to specific female friends on condition that the gifts were not to be controlled by their husbands. It revealed the feminist beliefs held by Eleanor – she regarded coverture as iniquitous. Throughout her business life she had shown real flair for controlling the whole manufacturing process – from the design to the making of the moulds, the making of the artificial stone, the carving and later the marketing and sale of finished items. By establishing links with all the leading architects of the day, and supplying stoneware to the most prestigious houses of the Georgian era, she cornered the market in her products. They were to be found at Carlton House, the Bank of England, and at the Royal Opera House. They appeared at the Royal Hospital at Chelsea, at Chiswick House and at Ham House in Richmond, and further north at Alnwick Castle in Northumberland, and Culzean Castle in Scotland; and every day, tens of thousands of people walk past the lion at Westminster Bridge, also made from Coade stone (see Plate 6).

Eleanor never patented the process, and for many years it was assumed that the formula had died with her. Remarkably, when the Coade factory closed the actual formula for her ceramic stone was forgotten. It has only recently been rediscovered. It reveals a complex mixture of different additives to what was termed 'ball clay' brought up from Dorset and Devon, including the intriguingly named 'grog'. This was pre-fired stoneware, ground up into a fine dust, and accounting for roughly 10 per cent of the final mix. The grog was mixed with sand, crushed soda lime glass, and pulverised flint grit. The mix was kneaded into a ball before being forced by hand into a pre-prepared mould. Baking in a kiln at very high temperatures (1,100 degrees) over a period of three to four days produced a ceramic-based stoneware, which was weatherproof and yet looked like the best quality limestone. Most significantly, the presence of the grog eliminated much of the shrinkage which was such a problem with earlier artificial stone. Eleanor's process reduced shrinkage in the kiln (and therefore distortion) from a massive 20 per cent to well under half that figure.

The product was a neutral, buff, colour, very similar to natural stone, and could be carved to a very sharp edge. It was possible for really fine details to be added after the firing process. It did not look glazed, but had a natural texture and matte finish, and most importantly, it was impervious to bad weather. Frost and ice do not damage it like limestone, and rain has little effect on it even after two centuries. It has survived in tombstones such as the one for Capability Brown. It has lasted indoors in mantle-pieces designed as faux wood, where wood could not have survived without scorching and splitting. It has been used as a base for statues submitted to a bronzing process – having been fired to such high temperatures it can be fired again with bronze, without cracking to make a product indistinguishable from solid metal.

So, what is to be made of Eleanor's legacy? She was an entrepreneur, a successful business woman, a person with a dogged nature and a good eye for profit. She embraced new ideas and exploited the opportunities which a changing world offered her. She blew wide open the myth that women could not run a successful manufacturing company, never once hiding behind the façade of male control. And yet … she was a one-off. No other artificial stone manufacturing company threatened her monopoly. No other Georgian businesswomen approached her in terms of acumen and business longevity, or came close to matching her success, and the question has to be asked: why ever not? Part of the answer must lie with women themselves – they chose not to follow her lead. It was not fashionable; it was not genteel. The attributes needed to be successful in business were seen as admirable in a man, but in a woman were dismissed as bossiness. The view of men is shown by Daniel Defoe in Moll Flanders:

> *'Tis evident that men can be their own advisors, and their own directors, and know how to work themselves out of difficulties and into business better than women.*

****

Men had long been used to forming clubs that excluded women, be they for business or pleasure. The first Grand Lodge of Freemasons was formed in 1717 with four lodges meeting at the Goose and Gridiron, in St Paul's Churchyard. Gentlemen joined men-only clubs where they could eat, drink, gamble and play cards, with 'White's' dating back to 1693. When two men were blackballed by White's, their rejection led to the formation of Boodle's (1762) and Brooks's (1764). Other clubs sprang up like mushrooms both in London and across the country, and the members were keen to keep out oiks, riff-raff – and women – at all costs. Many of the clubs were dominated by the two main political groups of the day, the Tories and the Whigs. As women could not vote, their involvement in political matters was peripheral and there was no perceived reason why they should be admitted as members.

Whereas men tried to exclude, women tended to join associations and groups which were open to both genders – salons, literary societies, and so on. It was not until another century had elapsed that the first women-only clubs appeared, with the Alexandra in 1884. This was decidedly for the upper echelons of society, i.e. women who were 'ladies of position'. The University Club was started in 1887 and membership was restricted to women who had been in residence for at least three terms in Girton or Newnham, Cambridge, or Lady Margaret or Somerville, Oxford. Formed in 1892, the Pioneer Club was a temperance society for women. A plethora of other female clubs were formed at the time of the First World War. The point is: in the eighteenth century there were no such groups, and therefore women in business were denied the opportunity of networking, which their male counterparts regarded as second nature. Similarly, there were no schools for girls offering the type of entry into the commercial, legal and political world to match Eton, Harrow and Rugby.

All this was happening at a time when the professions were closing ranks on outsiders, forming themselves into trade associations and institutes. Solicitors formed the Law Society in 1823. There were no women lawyers and therefore there was no need to have a constitution which permitted women to join. Other professions followed suit, all keen to maintain the *status quo*. The first female dentist was not enrolled until 1895

(Lilian Murray) and the first female architect was not admitted to the professional body until 1898 (Ethel Charles). In the judiciary we didn't get a female judge sitting at the Old Bailey until Rose Heilbron in January 1972 (although Elizabeth Lane had been made county court judge in 1962). The first female magistrate was Emily Dawson in 1913, and the first woman to be enrolled as a solicitor was Carrie Mason in 1922. The same year saw the first female surveyor appointed (Irene Barclay). Meanwhile, having qualified in America, Elizabeth Barrett became the first woman to have her name entered on the General Medical Council's medical register (1859). It was not until the 1870s that Oxford and Cambridge developed colleges for women, but whereas they could attend courses and take exams they were not allowed to matriculate, i.e. become graduate members of the university until 1920 and 1948 respectively. These milestones are given to emphasise that by abstaining from business, largely by their own volition in the 1700s, women then found their progress barred in the 1800s and it was not until the 1900s that these barriers were slowly and noisily dismantled.

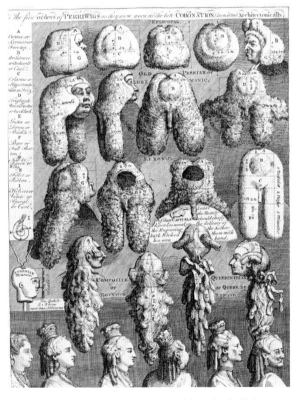

Hogarth's *Five Orders of Periwigs*: neither the Judiciary nor the Church were open to women.

Chapter 10

Mary Darly – print shop owner

It is a strange quirk of history that there is so little known about the life of Mary Darly; there is no record of when and where she was born, or married, or died – and yet she occupies a pivotal role in the evolution of caricatures. Her efforts, jointly with her husband, helped create the phenomenon of the print shop, a place where crowds clamoured to see the latest prints. Her premises were in all senses 'one-stop shops' – where the drawings were made, the copper engravings prepared, then printed, and then displayed for public consumption. The shops also sold artists materials such as stencils for use on silk, paper or linen; pastels; and ready-made paints. In addition, the Darlys offered lessons to the public in how to draw facial likenesses. Indeed, the public were encouraged to submit their drawings so that engravings could be prepared, and the resulting prints were then exhibited and offered for sale.

One exhibitor was the distinguished politician George, 4th Viscount and 1st Marquess of Townshend. A former soldier, Townshend impressed Horace Walpole, who wrote about him in 1757: 'His genius for likeness in caricatura is astonishing.' In 1756 the Darlys had begun publishing Townshend's drawings as small sixpenny prints, the size of playing cards. The first of these was *The Pillars of State*, satirising the Duke of Newcastle and Henry Fox, and the same year saw his much-discussed attack on the Duke of Cumberland, under the title of *Gloria Mundi*. For ten years from 1756, prints by Townshend and others were republished by Mary as pocket-sized annuals under the general title *A Political and Satyrical History of the Year*.... In time, the term 'caricature' came to be used to describe this type of political print.

Biographical details are few, but Mary is shown as flourishing between 1759 and 1781. However, it is difficult to distinguish between the achievements of Mary, and those of her husband Matthew Darly. Whereas in his early days as a printer of architectural books he had signed his plates as 'Matthew', 'Mathias' or 'Matt', by the time the husband and wife team moved into making fashion caricatures, both deliberately abbreviated their signatures to 'M Darly'. In effect, it was a recognition that they were a partnership of one – their individual contributions were indistinguishable and irrelevant.

There is one area where Mary's separate identity is apparent – in the advertisements for the business, which use words such as 'authoress' and 'inventress'. In 1762 Mary published the first manual on how to draw caricatures, under the title of *A Book*

of Caricaturas: on 59 Copper-Plates, with Ye Principles of Designing in that Droll &
Pleasing Manner, with Sundry Ancient & Modern Examples & Several Well Known
Caricaturas. It contained an introductory commentary of a single page, plus three
pages of instruction, followed by fifty-nine examples of face shapes. As the title page
stated, the book provided guidance in drawing caricatures and set out Mary's offer to
publicise the efforts of amateur artists: 'any carrick will be etched and published that
the Authoress shall be favoured with, Post paid'. 1762 also saw Mary referring to herself
as 'Fun Merchant, at the Acorn in Ryder's Court, Fleet Street.' Her own definition of
caricatures was that they were 'the burlesque of character, or an exaggeration of nature,
especially of those forms and features which have a striking peculiarity in them'.

Matthew had originally been involved in preparing copper plates for etchings
of technical drawings, for instance those used by Thomas Chippendale in his *The*
Gentleman and Cabinet-Maker's Director. He also came up with a number of ideas for
architectural features such as designs for ceilings and chimneys, and for furniture
inspired by the vogue for chinoiserie. By 1756 the Darlys were running a print shop in
Church Court opposite London's Hungerford Market, and within six years Mary had
her own shop in Ryders Court, Cranbourne Alley, near Leicester Fields. By 1765 the
couple had opened a third shop, at 39 the Strand. They all operated under the Sign of
the Acorn (or Golden Acorn). In time, the Darlys cornered the market in caricatures
satirising the macaroni movement. This was a spin-off from the aristocratic penchant
for going on the Grand Tour, bringing back from their travels a fashion for all things
Italian. Exaggerated wigs with long tails, quizzing glasses, long walking sticks, tightly
cut jackets and breeches – all accompanied by an effeminate style – made the macaroni
an easy target. Being '*à la macaroni*' affected not just clothing and hairstyles, but also
art and music. In 1764 the notorious gossip Horace Walpole made reference to '…the
Maccaroni Club (which is composed of all the travelled young men who wear long
curls and spying-glasses)…' and later expressed the view that the excesses of fashion
and coiffure were the result of too much money and not enough taste. A writer in the
Oxford Magazine commented in 1770:

There is indeed a kind of animal, neither male nor female, a thing of the neuter gender,
lately started up amongst us. It is called Macaroni. It talks without meaning, it smiles
without pleasantry, it eats without appetite, it rides without exercise, it wenches without
passion.

The Darlys were central to the public mockery of macaroni fashion and manners. They
published six series of twenty-four prints each between 1771 and 1773, showing how
macaroni-ism pervaded all classes. There was the macaroni soldier, dancing master, waiter

and artist, as well as the macaroni lawyer and clergyman. In 1772 there was even a print entitled *The Female Connoisseur* depicting Mary Darly examining a caricature sketch – presumably one of her own. In effect, this parody of fashion excess helped launch the later vogue for fashion plates in magazines such as *La Belle Assemblée*, giving examples of laudable fashion. It also helped to merge caricature with satire, laying the way for the ridicule dominating the works of men such as the acerbic James Gillray, and the ever-so-gentle Henry Bunbury, both of whom exhibited their works in the Darly shops.

In 1773 the Darlys held an exhibition of 233 original drawings for prints. Collected sets of the drawings had been offered for sale from 1772, feeding on the fashion for collecting accessible art. By then the Darlys had moved away totally from political satirical prints. As they made clear in the advertisements they warned that 'illiberal and indelicate Hints were not admissible', and that 'low or political Subjects will not be noticed'. Instead they wanted to promote 'laughable Subjects, droll Figures and sundry Characters'.

The Darly business appears to have come to a sudden end, probably through ill health. May 1779 saw the last advertisement for their comic prints. Later that year 'an extensive stock of prints and drawings, together with 1,200 copper plates … also, the household furniture fixtures and various effects, late the property of the well-known ingenious Mr Matt Darly, Printseller' were advertised for sale by public auction. Matthew died on 25 January 1780. His widow continued to sell prints, from 159 Fleet Street, for a two-year period. Her date of death is not known, but it was probably towards the end of 1781. By then the Darlys had established caricatures as a mainstream art form, collected by the rich, but also enjoyed by the poor and illiterate who eagerly pressed their noses against the shop window, anxious to share in the ridicule of the preposterous fashions and manners of the day (see Plate 8). Matthew and Mary may have morphed into 'M Darly', but together they changed the face of London in particular, and of society in general. Mary was an artist, an engraver, and a writer. She was also a print seller, publisher and teacher – and she gave the public what they wanted.

****

Mary was not, of course, the only woman running a print shop. She probably inspired her 'rival' Hannah Humphrey, who was more interested in the sales side of the operation. Hannah came from a family with a business selling seashells – popular with collectors of natural history items as well as with ladies who used the smaller shells to make pictures. Hannah's brother William had inherited the business but was more interested in preparing mezzotints and engravings based on Old Masters, rather than selling conches and cowries from the Shell Warehouse in St Martin's Lane. In 1774 he opened a print shop in Gerrard Street, selling 'drolls' and other engravings of a light-hearted nature, as well as his own mezzotints. By 1780 he had opened premises in the Strand, but apparently moved on to other interests, leaving his sister Hannah to develop the family print shop business. To begin with she purchased old engraving plates from elsewhere and simply 'doctored' the plates to show her name as publisher, but in time she started to commission and sell etchings from new engravings. Her shop at 18 Old Bond Street stocked portraits, historical scenes as well as caricatures. Clearly she had a knack of assessing public taste – and also of opening in premises which were certain to catch the eye of the buying public.

When the developing talent of one James Gillray started to attract attention, Hannah vied with the Darlys and the print seller Samuel Fores for the right to sell his etchings. Gillray was clever – he would produce near identical engravings of the same subject and sell exclusively to each shop. By 1791 Gillray had given up freelancing and produced prints for Hannah on an exclusive basis, no doubt helped by the fact that the artist moved in with her and lived 'above the shop'. New premises were acquired, and in 1797 they moved in to 27 St James's Street.

What is interesting is the way the caricature demonstrates that the prints appealed to all classes of society, with a posse of rich and poor peering in through the window. The poor thronged to see their social superiors pilloried for their mistakes and peccadilloes. The middle classes developed a liking for collecting prints on a regular basis, either to adorn their walls or to have bound up into volumes. The politicians, the statesmen and the royal princes were equally eager to come and see whether they were being lampooned, so there was no better place to exhibit the prints than in St James, just opposite clubs such as Boodles, White's and other places where the very people satirised by Gillray were likely to be found. Royalty was also involved, and in the case of the Prince of Wales, he is known to have bought over a 120 prints from Hannah Humphrey in the period between 1806 and 1807.

No doubt encouraged by Hannah, James Gillray was happy to lampoon Tory and Whig alike – both sold well to an eager public, and trade seemed to benefit from the 'even-handedness' of the vitriolic outpourings on display! Each new print generated a furore of interest, one anonymous witness writing in 1802 noting: 'The enthusiasm is indescribable when the next drawing appears; it is a veritable madness. You have to make your way in through the crowd with your fists.'

A year later another commented: 'The heads of the gazers before the shop-front of Mrs Humphrys were thrust one over another, and wedged so close, side by side, that… nothing could be more amusing than to listen to the remarks of the loitering crowd.'

Crowds gathering around the bow-fronted windows of Hannah's shop attracted less welcome followers of fashion. John Corry, writing in 1803, speaks of:

an authenticated fact, that girls often go in parties to visit the windows of printshops, that they may amuse themselves with the view of prints which impart the most impure ideas. Before these windows, the apprentice loiters – unmindful of his master's business; and thither prostitutes hasten, and with fascinating glances endeavour to allure the giddy and the vain who stop to gaze on the sleeping Venus; The British Venus, and a variety of seductive representations of naked feminine beauty.

The popularity spread to continental Europe, with the Weimar-based publication *London und Paris* regularly carrying commentaries written by their London correspondent Johann Christian Hüttner, and including details of the latest caricatures. In 1806 he wrote:

Caricature shops are always besieged by the public, but it is only in Mrs. Humphrey's shop where Gillray's works are sold, that you will find people of high rank, good taste and intelligence. This woman runs a successful business selling her own publications alone.

On another occasion the *London und Paris* noted: 'You will always see dozens of people standing outside the shops which sell these caricatures.'

It seems highly probable that Hannah used the same business connections established across the continent by her brother George, who sold shells and mineral curiosities throughout Europe. Particularly in the early stages of the French Revolution, Gillray titled his prints in both French and English, suggesting a deliberate attempt to service a market overseas. Later, as Gillray turned savagely against the French Revolution, and with war with France involving a trade embargo, such overseas sales diminished.

Hannah was canny enough to sell on a wholesale basis to the trade, as well as direct to the public. This is evidenced by the uproar which followed her publication of Gillray's print entitled *The Presentation, or, The Wise Men's Offering* in January 1796. It was considered blasphemous because it showed Fox and Sheridan fawning at the figure of Princess Charlotte, born a couple of days earlier, in a manner reminiscent of religious paintings such as *Adoration of the Magi*. James Gillray and Hannah Humphrey were arrested – along with a number of other print sellers such as Samuel Fores who can only have obtained the print for distribution on a wholesale basis from Hannah's shop. It is impossible to resist the conclusion that the pair 'cut a deal' – proceedings against Samuel Fores went ahead, whereas charges against James Gillray and Hannah Humphrey were dropped. Subsequently it emerged that Gillray was being paid a government pension, presumably for agreeing to toe the party line. It is fair to presume that Hannah was happy to influence her star exhibit to accept the government bribe. Business was business … and Hannah was nothing if not a shrewd businesswoman.

It is unclear how many were employed in the Humphrey emporium, but in all likelihood there would have been at least four men operating the two flatbed printing presses in the basement. One or more colourists would have been employed to finish off the prints, with colouring added by hand. Gillray himself liked to engrave his own copper plates, and there was at least one maid, the constant companion, Betty. Receipts signed by Gillray suggest that he may also have 'manned the fort', i.e. serving behind the counter if neither Hannah nor Betty were available.

Both Betty and Hannah are shown in Gillray's print *Two-Penny Whist* published in 1796 and showing the bespectacled Hannah looking on as Betty wins the trick with the Ace of Spades. (The print is shown as Plate 8.)

Despite living with James for many years, the couple never married, although it is reported that on one occasion they intended to wed. Getting as far as the gates of the church at St James's, Gillray had a change of heart and announced to Hannah: 'This is a foolish affair methinks, Miss Humphrey – we live very comfortably together, and we had better let well alone', and promptly went back to work. History does not record Hannah's views on the matter, but she nursed him through his latter years of mental illness and attempted suicide, and was bequeathed all his possessions when he died. Under the terms of his will made in 1807 (eight years before he died) Gillray left everything 'to my dearest friend Hannah Humphrey'.

Hannah, and before her, Mary Darly, were just two of many women engaged in the print trade, and they were most active when it was in its heyday. Earlier female successes include Anne Dodd, born around 1685 and dying in 1739. She had married the stationer Nathaniel Dodd in 1708 and, jointly with her husband, ran a business at the *Sign of the Peacock* at Temple Bar selling newspapers and pamphlets to the trade, and to the general public. The law of coverture meant that the business was conducted in Nathaniel's name, but when he died in 1723 Anne took over sole control and the business flourished for another sixteen years. She helped launch no fewer than six new periodicals, either on her own or in partnership with Elizabeth Nutt. Anne Dodd and Elizabeth Nutt may have been business rivals but they were also both members of a number of associations, known in the printing trades as 'congers', involving groups of printers combining forces to safeguard copyright and to publish books which might be too complex for any one person to handle. Congers offered an effective way of collective action, and many of the newspaper titles were owned via groups of shareholders pursuing a common goal. Sometimes these congers seemed to operate more on the side of anti-government publications, and on at least one occasion Anne Dodd was prosecuted; they appear to have been fearless and willing to oppose the government and to pursue demands for change. Elizabeth Nutt was imprisoned on numerous occasion, but in each case one or other of her daughters seems to have stepped in and continued publication on her behalf.

Known as 'mercuries', pamphlet sellers and newspaper printers such as Anne Dodd and Elizabeth Nutt represented the tip of an iceberg; below them were a host of female hawkers selling pamphlets on the streets. As a combination, they provided a network of news sellers throughout London, and occasionally further afield, based on loyalty and trust. For the government of the day these female groups must have appeared to be a many-headed Hydra, all parts solidly supporting the whole. The willingness of widows and daughters to step up to the plate when the male proprietor was imprisoned or died merely added to the inability of the government to act decisively when bringing prosecutions for libel, sedition and so on. Arguably, it was this solidarity which made it possible for later print shop owners, the Darlys and the Humphreys of the world, to flourish without generally being molested through the courts. Instead, politicians and royalty alike dipped into their pockets and paid them to go away.

A MACARONI. PRINTSELLER.

A Macaroni Printseller by M Darly.

Chapter 11

Teresia 'Con' Phillips – bigamist, litigant and courtesan

Teresia Constantia Phillips, known generally as 'Con', was a remarkable figure. Born in 1709 in Chester she moved to London with her parents, but left home after her mother died. Her father chose to marry his servant, and Teresia was bullied and abused by her new stepmother. At the age of 12 she went to live in lodgings, where she was befriended by a young man called Thomas Grimes (actually a pseudonym for a young aristocrat, originally believed to have been Philip Stanhope, 4th Earl of Chesterfield, but now generally thought to have been Thomas Lumley-Saunderson, 3rd Earl of Scarbrough). Regardless of the identity of her assailant, she was plied with Barbados Water (i.e. rum), raped and then abandoned. She trod the well-worn path into child prostitution, running up debts of £500 by the time she was 14, due to her propensity for buying fine silks and expensive gowns at exorbitant interest rates. Knowing that marriage would transfer those debts to a husband, she was then persuaded by friends to pay a man called Delafield to go through a form of marriage ceremony. In fact, he was already married and was a professional bigamist – in other words he accepted money in return for going through with a marriage ceremony officiated by the notorious Fleet parson Revd John Draper. The groom was three sheets to the wind, and after the ceremony he was put to bed, utterly comatose, so that his new 'bride' could slip between the sheets. Her friends then trooped in to witness the fact that consummation had taken place.

A sham marriage such as this was often used to put creditors off the scent – the onus would be on creditors to show that the marriage was genuine if they sought to pursue Delafield through the courts for Teresia's debts. In fact, within a very few months, Teresia met and fell for the charms of a Dutch merchant by the name of Henry Muilman. He proposed marriage, and the wedding took place at the identical church to the previous ceremony, in February 1724. She was thus 15 at the time of her second 'marriage'. When the Muilman family heard of the new bride's notorious past they persuaded their son to apply for the marriage to be declared null and void – the start of a litigation process which would be spread over two decades and which would not be resolved until 1748. Muilman had little choice, as it was made clear to him that he would never be allowed to inherit his father's considerable fortune unless he 'got rid of' his embarrassment of a wife. The problem was that Teresia preferred to retain her married status, and had no wish to see the ceremony annulled and her debts returned to her own doorstep.

Suffice to say that Teresia took the opportunity of the confusion over her marital status to pursue a very considerable number of bedroom conquests, generally involving the aristocracy. This in turn funded an extravagant lifestyle, and she always insisted on the best box at the theatre, the finest clothes, and the most expensive jewels.

She also developed a thriving business at the *Sign of the Green Canister* in Covent Garden's Half Moon Street, where ladies (and gentlemen) could buy those items which were so useful in her line of business – sex toys such as dildos (otherwise known as *consolateurs* or *godemiches*) and condoms, generally referred to as 'machines'.

Her tumultuous relationship with Mr Muilman continued to rumble along sporadically. He seemed hell-bent on giving up the status of marriage but rather less keen on relinquishing his conjugal rights. Indeed, it seems likely that her lawyers encouraged her to permit these sexual encounters; after all, she was contending that she was properly married to Muilman, and therefore he had every right to her body. But Teresia claimed that Muilman bullied and mistreated her, on one occasion branding her with a hot poker and, on another, hiring 'ruffians' to attack her, steal all her clothes and jewellery, and cast her out into the street in the middle of winter, clad only in an under shift.

What made the story remarkable was that Teresia never threw in the towel, never wavered in her determination to get her own back. She published her *Apology*, justifying her conduct, as an eighteen-part serial, later bound up as three volumes, while the litigation was still unresolved. It was in all likelihood used as a deliberate ploy to blackmail her various lovers into paying her to be silent. It gives a rollicking read as it lists her conquests and details the legal chicanery and outright dishonesty of the lawyers who made their money out of litigants such as her. Deliberate suppression of court records, the fabrication of false statements, general procrastination and very possibly the murder of Mr Delafield, the main witness, were but some of the tricks which Teresia claimed were employed by Muilman's legal team. The spin-off of the original suit in nullity took Teresia before the London Consistory Court, the Court of Arches, the Court of Delegates and Kings Bench and Chancery. Never once did she flinch from addressing her cause before the highest judges in the land. She was determined to show that she was the victim in all that had happened, and that it was unfair that the original rape should mean that her subsequent actions were seen in such a poor light by society. She maintained that it was the rape which precipitated all her subsequent misfortunes.

As the victim of the rape, why should she be blamed? Why should she not seek to support herself in whatever way she could?

The challenge before the courts was to establish the validity of not one but three different marriage ceremonies: the original one by Delafield; his subsequent 'marriage' to Teresia, and thereafter her marriage to Muilman. After all, if the first ceremony was invalid for any reason – e.g. because Delafield's bride was already married – then the second ceremony (Delafield/Phillips) was good and the third would be bigamous. On the other hand, if the first marriage was sound, the second was null and void on account of Delafield's bigamy, and in that case Teresia would be left with a perfectly valid wedding to Muilman.

Why was it important? Because bigamy was potentially a capital offence, at least until the 1790s when the punishment was replaced with transportation for a seven-year period. In practice bigamy was a relatively common offence, sometimes involving quite unwitting parties. If the marriage of a working-class couple broke down there was no question of getting a divorce, they simply went their separate ways. With no national register of marriages and deaths it was almost impossible to ascertain whether a person was free to marry after a few years had passed. But a court verdict of bigamy would have been a real kick in the teeth for Teresia. With it she would lose her thin veneer of respectability, her ability to pass her bills on to Muilman, and her immunity from liabilities linked to the shop business. She fought tooth and nail to stay married, despite her obvious adultery and generally promiscuous behaviour. Men could have it both ways, why couldn't she?

It is worth considering why Muilman did not opt for a divorce rather than an annulment. The answer was simple: divorce was a rich man's game, and an extremely rare one at that, involving a Bill being put before Parliament, giving members of both Houses the chance to see and hear all the details of the couple's misfortunes.

Teresia eventually finished her fight for justice and set sail for New England and later settled in Jamaica, There she showed that she had not lost her appetite, either for men or for marriage. She wed three men, all bigamously, in quick succession. Her husbands conveniently proved to be very short-lived after marriage, each dying within months. Each left their estate to Teresia. She was a well-known figure on the island and was soon given the moniker 'The Black Widow'. Life was lived to the full by the hedonistic plantation owners, echoing the sort of excess seen 150 years later in Kenya's Happy Valley, and Teresia played her part to the full. She was eventually appointed Mistress of the Revels, a post which paid her a small amount of money. It was an unofficial position which entailed presiding over street festivals held in Spanish Town, and it is likely that she also had a say in deciding which plays were performed in Jamaican playhouses. She needed the money, because by then she had spent all her savings and inheritances, and she died, un-mourned and in debt, aged 56, in February 1765.

What comes across was not so much a serial bigamist and courtesan, as a woman with an implacable feeling of injustice. She knew the law was corrupt. She knew that society was hypocritical and stacked against the rights of women. She railed against those injustices and in the end used marriage to get her own back on a world which rushed to pass judgment on the victim of rape, rather than on the perpetrator of the crime. As she said in her *Apology*, her story was a cautionary tale for all young ladies: 'A Woman may want conjugal Affection, Integrity, Sobriety, maternal Tenderness, Frugality, Good-Nature, Patience, Temperance, Prudence, Charity, and … every social Virtue, if she contrive to keep her Person chaste … all is well in the World's Opinion.'

Teresia may seem an odd choice among other business women of the eighteenth century – but that is the whole point; if a woman had entrepreneurial skills, one of the few businesses she could operate in was likely to be linked to the sex trade. The brothel owners and the courtesans enjoyed an elevated status as never before – they were the first 'celebrities' and the fashion icons of the day. Another point: Teresia Phillips had incredible tenacity and determination. She was absolutely convinced that her second marriage was legal, and no amount of lying, cheating, manipulating or prevaricating by her husband – and his lawyers – was going to put her off. She was absolutely determined to pursue her marital rights through every court in the land, whatever the cost to her and to any reputation that she might have had.

****

The perseverance through the courts by Teresia Phillips helped inspire some of the ideas of Jeremy Bentham, one of the greatest jurists, philosophers and social reformers of the eighteenth century. He claimed that he owed his zeal as a law reformer to the fact that 'Chance threw into my hand … in 1759, a precious autobiography … of the then celebrated courtesan, Teresia Constantia Phillips.' He went on to describe her as 'the fair penitent' tossed from pillar to post both by the law and the judiciary. The arcane procedures were seen by Bentham as 'this griping … screwing … eviscerating' process. He said that reading Teresia's story was to reveal 'the Daemon of Chicane … in all his hideousness. What followed? I abjured his empire. I vowed war against him. My vow has been accomplished'.

Bentham certainly saw Teresia as a victim. Her battle cry that 'the injured have a right to complain' struck a chord with many, even though she was pilloried in contemporary newspapers, plays and books. She was attacked for her avarice in bleeding her aristocratic lovers dry and then leaving them when they had run out of money and were unable to buy her yet more presents. But above all she was attacked for her rampant sexual appetite, her very obvious love of sex. Others might have forgiven her a single act of revenge against the man who raped her, or against the husband who misused her, but few could tolerate her brazen sexuality. She herself justified her openness as a sign of her integrity – she felt she had nothing to hide. She went on to complain that it was wrong that once a woman was debauched every man thinks 'he has a Right to demand the Possession of her Person, upon the same base Terms with the first'. And no, it wasn't right to blame a mistress for the financial ruin of her lovers – any more than you would blame the bottle, or the pack of playing cards which, as often as not, were the real cause of a man's downfall. If men were weak and extravagant, they should take the blame, not the woman.

Her twenty years of litigation also pushed Lord Hardwicke, before whom Teresia appeared in court on several occasions, to propose a complete overhaul of the way in which marriages were conducted and recorded. The Marriage Act of 1753 was the consequence, aimed at abolishing sham and clandestine weddings and putting the arrangements on a proper footing. It also established that parties to a marriage could always apply to have the marriage annulled, no matter what time had elapsed, if the wedding was based upon false information about the age, identity, or status of either the bride or the groom. Teresia might not have appreciated the irony, but by inspiring Hardwicke's Marriage Act her story led to the end of Fleet Marriages, the rise of Gretna Green as a wedding venue (because the new law did not apply to Scotland) and the beginning of state registration of weddings.

Eighteenth-century marriage vows.

Chapter 12

Elizabeth Raffald – cookery book writer and businesswoman

Born Elizabeth Whittaker in December 1733 there was little to mark out the daughter of a Doncaster schoolteacher as a future entrepreneur, writer and successful businesswoman. Her father presumably managed to instil a modicum of learning into her before she left home at 15 to work as a housekeeper for a succession of Yorkshire families. She progressed to working for Sir Peter and Lady Elizabeth Warburton at Arley, near Northwich, Cheshire, helping in the kitchens of Arley Hall. She spent the next fifteen years there, learning her trade as a cook and, more importantly, learning what it took to run the business side of looking after the eating requirements of a wealthy household.

She fell for the charms of John Raffald, one of the gardeners at Arley Hall, and in March 1763 the couple were married. As was customary at the time, this involved moving out from her place of employment to reflect her change in status as a married woman, and the couple moved to John's hometown of Manchester. At that stage it had not yet become the steam-driven urbanisation nicknamed 'Cottonopolis', but it was already a prosperous town benefiting from the plethora of cotton mills constructed along the banks of the rivers Irwell and Mersey, Medlock and Irk. The mills brought wealth – not just to the mill owners and their managers, but to the builders of their fine houses and of their factories – cathedrals of industrial might and power. The merchants importing ever-increasing numbers of bales of cotton into Manchester, alongside vast quantities of sugar from the Caribbean, grew rich (much of it on the back of the slave trade). These merchants, industrialists and speculators had large disposable incomes and an appreciation of fine things – and Elizabeth was determined to give them what they wanted.

In particular, many of these newly rich came from households unused to entertaining. Elizabeth must have had her hands full with a young family – some reports suggest that she had nine, or even fifteen or sixteen children, but sadly only three survived. However, in between bringing up these children she opened a confectionary store in Fennel Street, alongside a school teaching cookery to young women. 'Confectionary' meant rather more than selling sweets; she was more analogous to the French *traiteur* providing pre-prepared meals, or parts of meals, on a take-out basis. She sold cooked meats, and soups, as well as providing foodstuffs associated with a modern delicatessen. In addition to supplying cooked food and table centrepieces, she delivered dried goods such as tea and coffee throughout the Salford neighbourhood. As she said in her advertisement in the *Manchester Mercury* of 29 November 1763, she could supply 'Cold Entertainments, Hot French Dishes, Confectionaries, &c.' Meanwhile her husband, who was already showing a propensity for drinking any profits from the business, sold vegetables at a stall in the market and may have had an interest in a florist shop nearby.

Elizabeth branched out into running an employment agency for household servants, matching up employers with those eager for work in 'the big houses up on the hill'. It is believed to have been the first of its kind in Manchester. In September 1766 she moved her business to Exchange Alley near the Bull's Head in the Market Place (later to become the Exchange Coffee House). She increasingly used local newspapers to promote her business and by 1768, her advertisements in the *Manchester Mercury* were referring to the availability of 'creams, possets, jellies, flummery and lemon cheese cakes'. She also advised the public that she could supply 'plumb cakes for weddings' – the earliest reference to wedding cake. As the advertisement put it:

> *Mrs. Raffald returns thanks for the great encouragement she meets with in making Bride and Christening Cakes and those who are pleased to favour her with their commands, may depend on being served with such cakes as shall not be exceeded.*

Four years later, she decided that Manchester and Salford could do with a trade directory to reflect the burgeoning growth of the city. It showed where everyone lived, on a street-by-street basis. The 1772 edition sold well and was immediately updated, expanded and republished in 1773 and again in 1781. Clearly interested in the power and influence of local newspapers, she helped to establish Salford's first newspaper, called *Prescott's Journal,* and acquired part-ownership in *Harrop's Mercury.*

Because of the law of coverture the businesses were conducted in her husband's name. John was more interested in hanging out with his drinking buddies and decided to run a coaching inn at The King's Head in Chapel Street. This involved hiring out carriages and, for Elizabeth, catering for the Officer's Mess. The stage to London ran from the King's Head, and Elizabeth also started a post office at the premises. The business foundered, whereupon John obtained a licence at the Exchange, where once more Elizabeth did the catering. She also ran a stall supplying refreshments at Kersal Races.

Under the guidance of Charles White, who helped found Manchester Royal Infirmary, she started writing a book on midwifery, but it was never finished and no trace of it remains. At the age of 48, Elizabeth suffered a spasm and died suddenly. She was buried at Stockport Parish Church, and immediately afterwards John's creditors moved in on him and seized his goods.

So far, this has been a story of an innovative and astute business woman, who kept coming up with money-making ideas, but who ultimately did not achieve more because of her husband's problem with the demon drink. But there was rather more to Elizabeth Raffald – and the reason why she is remembered today, and why the National Portrait Gallery in London has two portraits of her: she wrote a cookery book.

Up until that time cookery books were largely derivative of other books, using pirated recipes, and frequently borrowing heavily on French terms and ideas on cooking. In 1769 she published, in Manchester, her book *The Experienced English Housekeeper*. It retailed at five shillings and ran to 800 copies, each of them signed personally by Elizabeth to prevent further pirating. The book was dedicated to Lady Elizabeth Warburton, her employer at Arley Hall, and contained some 800 recipes.

Two years later the book was republished through R. Baldwin of 47 Paternoster Row in London. Again, each of the 400 copies was signed personally. Further reprints followed in 1775 (with the addition of an extra 100 recipes) and 1778. By 1784 there were no fewer than thirteen legal editions of the book, but by then pirated versions had come off the presses – some twenty-one of them. A special edition adapted for the American market came out posthumously in 1801.

The book was aimed at cooks working for the newly prosperous families in Manchester and beyond. It was for novices, using basic cooking methods, but it was particularly for aspirational novices – those who wanted to learn how to produce meals for 'fine dining'. As Elizabeth said in a note to Lady Warburton, 'I am not vain enough to propose adding anything to the experienced housekeeper, but hope these recipes may be of use to young persons who are willing to improve themselves.'

It reflected 'modern' ideas, or as she stated, '[I] have made it my Study to set out the Dinner in as elegant a Manner as lies in my Power, and in the Modern Taste.' One of the recipes included bride cake, using almond paste and royal icing. The book also included what is believed to be the first recipe for what we would recognise as Eccles Cake, using flaky pastry instead of yeast.

The book was divided into three sections:

Part First: Lemon Pickle, Browning for all Sorts of Made Dishes, Soups, Fish, plain Meat, Game, Made Dishes both hot and cold, Pyes, Puddings, &c,
Part Second: All Kind of Confectionary, particularly the Gold and Silver Web for covering of Sweetmeats, and a Desert of Spun Sugar, with Directions to set out a Table

in the most elegant Manner and in the modern Taste, Floating Islands, Fish Ponds, Transparent Puddings, Trifles, Whips, &c.
Part Third: *Pickling, Potting, and Collaring, Wines, Vinegars, Catchups, Distilling, with two most valuable Receipts, one for refining Malt Liquors, the other for curing Acid Wines, and a correct List of every Thing in Season in every Month of the year.*

Illustrations were used to show how dishes were to be displayed on the table. In 1773 Elizabeth sold her copyright in the book to her publisher, receiving the sum of £1,400. Using the retail price index this equates to a modern equivalent of perhaps £170,000 but in terms of buying power it is perhaps worth closer to more than £3 million. She was famous, and she was wealthy. Her portrait appears in Plate 9, holding out a copy of the cookery book by which she is remembered.

****

Her achievements, and legacy, should be seen in context. She was not, for instance, the first woman to write a successful cookery book. Before her was Hannah Glasse, whose book *The Art of Cookery made Plain and Easy* came out in 1747, and was described as having been written 'by a Lady'. According to James Boswell, Samuel Johnson was familiar with the book but was convinced that it was penned by a man, apparently remarking: 'Women can spin very well; but they cannot make a good book of cookery.' It became a bestseller for almost 100 years, running through over forty separate editions. But Elizabeth Raffald was proud of her roots. She did not publish anonymously or claim to be 'a lady'. She used her own name and happily informed the whole world where she had worked and gained the knowledge to write the book. She was also proud of her northern origins, declining to alter north-country expressions when her London publisher asked her to tone down her dialect.

Elizabeth Raffald was also not the only person to bring new tastes and products to the attention of the public, as evidenced by the activities of Mrs Clements of Durham. She was the widow of a local miller, and some time before 1720 she decided to apply the same method of milling mustard seeds as had been used to make superfine flour from wheat – in other words by separating out and discarding all the stalks, leaves and the outer husks, before grinding the mustard to a fine powder. Prior to that time the whole plant was ground up, usually in a pestle and mortar, but by giving it 'the full works', Mrs Clements came up with a much hotter taste than had ever previously been obtained. She brought her product to London where it became a great favourite of George I. When Mrs Clements died, the recipe passed to her daughter. She was married to a Joseph William Ainsley and he carried on mustard milling from premises in Silver Street, Durham. Soon, competitors appeared on the scene and they copied the milling method of producing hot mustard, including the business of Messrs Keen & Son in London. By 1742 they were using the expression 'keen as mustard' in their advertising. Eventually all these smaller businesses were absorbed within the Colman's empire, thereby moving mustard production from Durham to Colman's headquarters in Norwich towards the end of the reign of George III.

Elizabeth Raffald was also not the first woman to realise the potential of provincial newspapers and print businesses. In the 140 years following 1700 there were apparently some 59 women who headed print businesses in the North and North East of the country – all of them via an inheritance either from a father or husband. And she certainly was not the first to help run a tavern. Indeed, this was traditionally the work of women, as was brewing the actual beer being sold. In a tradition going back centuries, and reflected in today's microbreweries, each tavern would make its own beers for consumption on the premises. As often as not, it was the woman who was the brewster.

Most obviously, Elizabeth Raffald was not the first woman to run shop premises under the name of a husband. One of the great hallmarks of the eighteenth century was the appearance of a middle class, and much of that new class was made up of successful retail traders. The century made Britain a nation of shopkeepers. This was not a phrase originated by Napoleon Bonaparte, as is popularly supposed, but by the economist Adam Smith. In *The Wealth of Nations* (1776) he wrote:

> *To found a great empire for the sole purpose of raising up a people of customers may at first sight appear a project fit only for a nation of shopkeepers. It is, however, a project altogether unfit for a nation of shopkeepers; but extremely fit for a nation whose government is influenced by shopkeepers.*

Subsequently it was used in a derogatory sense by the French revolutionary Bertrand Barère de Vieuzac. On 11 June 1794 he addressed the National Convention with the words: 'Let Pitt then boast of his victory to his nation of shopkeepers' – meaning that the English were no good at soldiering, merely at being tradesmen.

Trade was at the heart of Britain's success. As Napoleon is supposed to have confided to his surgeon O'Meara while exiled on St Helena, '…all your great riches, and your grand resources arose from commerce … What else constitutes the riches of England. It is not extent of territory, or a numerous population. It is not mines of gold, silver, or diamonds.'

What Elizabeth Raffald showed was that trade involved women just as much as men, even if a male name appeared over the shop door and on public registers. Mind you,

Daniel Defoe would have us believe that the men stayed at home to work (tradesmen did not typically 'go out' to work) whereas women did their bit for trade by going out to spend the money men had made. Writing in *The Complete English Tradesman* Defoe states:

> *it is apparent, that the expensive living of most tradesmen in their families, is for want of a serious acquainting their wives with their circumstances, and acquainting them also in time; for there are very few ladies so unreasonable, who, if their husbands seriously informed them how things stood with them, and that they could not support their way of living, would not willingly come into measures to prevent their own destruction....*
>
> *Indeed, I might have added here, that trade itself in England is not, as it generally is in other countries, the meanest thing the men can turn their hand to; but, on the contrary, trade is the readiest way for men to raise their fortunes and families; and, therefore, it is a field for men of figure and of good families to enter upon.*

The same book is crystal clear – businesses fail where businessmen trade beyond their stock, or give too much credit. Defoe particularly warned against going into debt and then over-borrowing:

> *Interest-money eats deep into the tradesman's profits, because it is a payment certain, whether the tradesman gets or loses .... The lender calls for his money when he pleases, and often comes for it when the borrower can ill spare it; and then, having launched out in trade on the supposition of so much in stock, he is left to struggle with the enlarged trade with a contracted stock, and thus he sinks under the weight of it, cannot repay the money, is dishonoured, prosecuted, and at last undone, by the very loan which he took in to help him.*

He might also have added that drinking the profits was not a good idea, but then, one suspects that John Raffald would not have bothered to read that particular chapter....

On the subject of shopping it is worth remembering that in the eighteenth century, shops were generally known as 'warehouses', i.e. places where wares were housed. 'Shopping' was a comparatively recent expression. The Oxford Dictionary (online) gives us this:

> *The earliest shops were small stalls or booths, like the ones you might see today in a market or used by a pavement trader. 'Shop' came into English as a medieval shortening of early French eschoppe 'lean-to booth'. The activity of shopping dates from the 1760s.*

Ask a woman in 1700 if she was going to visit a shop and she might assume that you meant visiting a prison, since that was its colloquial meaning. She would have regarded her activity in going out to buy items as 'marketing', i.e. in the sense of going to the market. It is however undeniable that, stripped of the ability to be educated and to hold down a job, many wives of wealthy husbands had little choice but to spend their time meeting up with other women and then heading off to spend the family fortunes. The economy needed wealth creators, but it also needed consumers and the adage that 'men created wealth, women spent it' may have been grossly unfair, but it was not entirely untrue, at least within the retail context.

A Milliner's Shop.

Chapter 13

Anna Fry – chocolatier

Anna Fry, who went on to head the country's largest firm of chocolate manufacturers in the last decade of the century, was born Anna Portsmouth in 1719. She was fortunate to be part of a well-to-do Quaker family who believed in female education and gender equality. Her father Henry was an apothecary, an eminent physician living in Basingstoke, and he took on as an apprentice a young Quaker called Joseph Fry. In particular, Joseph was able to learn about the medicinal properties of various plants and herbs. He was seven years younger than Anna and when he qualified as a doctor he moved to Bristol. Two years later, in 1755, he returned to Basingstoke to marry Anna, and together they made their home in Bristol. Neither had any particular connection with the city, but the family's success is a testament to the network of Quaker-based connections operating throughout the country. It was a network which he strengthened and developed during his thirty-two years in the city.

Joseph was a man of remarkable talent and enthusiasm. He had been born in Sutton Benger in Wiltshire and as a boy had been sent away to boarding school in the North of England. Like many Quakers who felt constrained by all the things that they were *not* allowed to do, he channelled all his energies into pursuing the opportunities which were open to him. As a Quaker he could not go to university, or rather, he could attend lectures but never matriculate. He could never vote or stand for Parliament, and many doors were closed to him because of his beliefs. Quakers believed that 'your word was your bond'. Truth was absolute, and that there were no degrees of truth. Swearing to something, or entering into a written promise, was meaningless if you had already given your word. The Quakers therefore fell foul of the Test Acts, passed in the aftermath of the restoration of the monarchy, requiring people to swear an Oath of Allegiance to the Crown. This discriminatory piece of legislation was designed to ensure that only adherents to the Church of England could gain public office. It was aimed against Roman Catholics but was effective at making life extremely difficult for other religious sects, including the Quakers. This prejudice and lack of opportunity spurred Joseph on. He developed a successful medical practice in Bristol, but really only continued with it as a basis for charitable works. His real interest was as an entrepreneur, developing business opportunities in his new home city. Chocolate manufacture, china production, typesetting foundries, and soap boiling/candle making were all business interests which he developed in Bristol, usually with Quaker partners.

The interest in chocolate arose out of the fact that chocolate was enjoyed for its medicinal properties – it was never a mere piece of confectionary. It was thought to be beneficial for people as an aphrodisiac (but curiously, also as a means of reducing stress and anxiety) and as an aid to fertility in women. It was, however, a treatment aimed at the wealthy, with chocolate being sold for 7s 6d per lb in the 1760s. That was roughly the equivalent to what an agricultural worker would earn in a whole week. The manufacturing process was time-consuming and complicated, involving the slow roasting of the beans over charcoal, followed by hand winnowing to remove the husks, and then the crushing of the cocoa beans by hydraulic rollers operating over a heated milling table. The cocoa mass was then heated, mixed with various herbs and spices such as cloves and cinnamon, along with other ingredients including sugar. Potassium carbonate or sodium would be added in small quantities to make it easier to dissolve, in a process known as 'dutching'. The mixture was then allowed to dry in small, pastille-shaped containers. The purchaser of this delicacy would then make a chocolate drink from the pastille, by adding hot milk (and sometimes other flavourings, including brandy). It was a method of production patented in 1729 by Walter Churchman, a Quaker pharmacist in Clifton, Bristol.

There are records suggesting that Joseph was experimenting with chocolate manufacture as early as 1759, from premises in Small Street. When Walter Churchman died he left his business to his son Charles, who lived until 1761. One of his executors was a John Vaughan, and he and Joseph Fry purchased the business from the estate. Operating as Fry, Vaughan & Co, they moved operations to Narrow Wine Street and then, in 1777, to nearby Union Street, right in the heart of the city. Joseph was constantly seeking to improve production techniques and endlessly experimented with the ingredients. Trade flourished, not least because the factory was close to the nearby town of Bath, with its hoards of aristocratic and well-heeled visitors. Within a few years the company had agents in over fifty towns throughout the country and had established a warehouse in London.

That was not the end of Joseph's business interests; he liked investing in new technologies and in established businesses where the opportunity for improved methods of production existed. In 1768 he invested £1,500 in the china clay manufactory of Richard Champion. He formed Fry, Fripp & Co to develop a soap-boiling business. In 1764 he went into partnership with Mr Pine, who printed the *Bristol Gazette*, to develop a type foundry and to produce new typefaces. This became a separate business, known initially as J Fry & Co and then as Joseph Fry & Co, and in 1782 Joseph took his two sons Henry and Edmund into partnership, and the printing arm of the business was particularly involved in producing Bibles. In 1785 the company brought out *A Specimen of Printing Types made by Joseph Fry & Sons, Letter-founders and Marking Instrument Makers by the King's Royal Letters Patent*.

Joseph died after a short illness in March 1787 at the age of 59. Edmund and Henry carried on with the typesetting business, but the chocolate manufacturing side of things was left to Anna. Her younger son, Joseph Storrs Fry, was just 18 when his father died, too young to be in charge of the company. So Anna stepped in and became the matriarchal head of the family business, which she ran as 'Anna Fry & Son' until her death in 1803 at the age of 83, although day-to-day control passed to her son in 1795. Under her auspices the company bought the first steam-powered cocoa grinding mill, designed by James Watt, and installed in the Bristol premises in 1795. This in turn led to modern methods of factory production.

Following her death, Anna's son Joseph Storrs Fry inherited the business, changed the business name, and eventually took his three sons into partnership, and called it 'J. S. Fry & Sons'. At that stage the company enjoyed a dominant share in the market, importing more than 40 per cent of all cocoa products in the country – a position which was gradually whittled away thanks to the more aggressive marketing strategies of those other Quaker chocolatiers, the Rowntrees and the Cadburys.

*****

Anna is interesting because she was at the helm for nearly fifteen years. She demonstrated the depth of experience and skills needed to preserve the family firm, and the success of the company is a reminder of just how many Quaker-owned companies came to dominate the marketplace in luxury goods. There was a certain irony in this given that Quakers did not allow ostentation or frivolous luxury.

In a sense Anna Fry was not a 'first', because she was one of many Quaker females who reaped the advantage of a good education, a close support network, sound financial knowledge and a good sense of knowing what the market wanted. But she deserves to be remembered simply because she was typical – she wasn't 'the one and only', she was one of many Quaker women who quietly went about their business, transforming society by their example. Quaker women were preachers (one of the few faiths to permit 'tub thumpers'). They became missionaries; they founded and ran schools; they instilled business ethics in their young charges; they participated in meetings discussing workers living conditions and helped implement calls for better housing, and for wages which were not just a minimum, but which provided a living wage (often 50 per cent more than was customary). At all levels, Quakerism used its tentacles to promote ideas of equality and freedom. It was therefore instrumental in bringing change – with the abolition of slavery, with schooling for all, with the growth of 'consensus politics' in the boardroom, and with the introduction of improved living conditions among the poor and disenfranchised.

A female 'tub-thumper' – a preacher at a Quaker Meeting.

Part Four

REFORMERS AND EDUCATIONALISTS

Paradigm:
Women have neither the ability nor opportunity for Influence.

A woman's power to influence – a curtain lecture!

Chapter 14

Margaret, Lady Middleton – anti-slavery campaigner

In a way, Margaret, Lady Middleton, achieved nothing out of the ordinary – she was an accomplished portrait artist; she was a close friend of Dr Johnson and David Garrick; she knew an awful lot of important people; and she held dinner parties. But she was also an extremely influential figure in the abolition movement, which perhaps explains why the Moravian preacher Christian Latrobe, a family friend, once claimed that 'the abolition of the slave trade was … the work of a woman, even Lady Middleton'. Later, in 1791, her friend Hannah More, herself a staunch abolitionist, wrote to Margaret saying 'you have the first title to every prize on the whole slave subject'. Praise indeed – and that from a woman very much involved in the behind-the-scenes work to promote the abolitionist cause.

For such an influential and fiercely intelligent woman there are remarkably few details of her early life. Born Margaret Gambier some time after 1730 into a family who had come to Britain as Huguenot refugees in the 1690s, she was well educated, clever and artistic. Her father, James Gambier, was married to Mary Mead. Her family were evangelical Christians, who saw it as their job to improve conditions in the world around them. If there was a wrong, then it was their Christian duty to right it. The fact that Margaret was a woman, and therefore had no prospect of going to university or entering Parliament, simply strengthened her view that her skill should lie in influencing others. She could not vote, but in her middle age she certainly learned how to persuade, cajole and inspire others to vote with their conscience.

Many would argue that Margaret was the single most influential person in persuading William Wilberforce to present the abolitionist case in Parliament. Not a naturally decisive man, he suffered constantly from self-doubt and needed the encouragement from Margaret to adopt the cause as his life's work. Wilberforce was not over-keen on allowing women to take part in the abolitionist meetings or to drum up support for petitions, writing in 1826:

I own I cannot relish the plan. All private exertions for such an object become their characteristic but for ladies to meet, to publish, to go from house to house stirring up petitions – these appear to me proceedings unsuited to the female character as delineated in Scripture. I fear its tendency would be to mix them all in the multiform warfare of political life.

The fact that the influence of Margaret Middleton was so effective is revealed in one of Wilberforce's letters to her, when he replies to her letter urging him to present a Bill before Parliament with the words: 'I feel the great importance of the subject and I think myself unequal to the task allotted to me, but yet I will not positively decline it.'

More importantly, once Wilberforce had committed himself to the cause, Margaret was closely involved in much of the strategic planning behind the various anti-slavery bills put before Parliament.

How did this happen? Largely in conjunction with her husband, whom she had met on her uncle's ship when he was in his mid-teens. A few years older than her, he was an impoverished servant working for Captain Samuel Mead, who was in charge of HMS *Sandwich*. The fact that she fell head-over-heels for him did not endear their relationship to her parents – his prospects were far from clear, and he had yet to establish a name for himself in his chosen career, i.e. the Royal Navy. She faced more parental opposition when she declined to marry a suitor of her parent's choice, and in time her parents disinherited her. The couple had to wait a further twenty years, until 1761, before the 35-year-old Charles Middleton was able to take a period of shore leave, and marry Margaret. She got pregnant immediately and gave birth to a daughter exactly nine months later.

In the period leading up to her marriage Margaret was estranged from her parents and lived with a close friend Elizabeth Bouverie, a Huguenot who owned an estate at Barham Court at Teston in Kent. Margaret and Elizabeth had been at school together, fostering a lifelong friendship. Together they had hosted parties for their artist friends and intellectuals – men like Samuel Johnson, who described Margaret as one of the wisest people he knew, and fellow artist Joshua Reynolds.

So close was the connection, and so generous was Elizabeth as host, that Margaret continued to live at Barham Court after she married. Eventually, the estate was bequeathed to Charles Middleton, and in 1761 Charles was happy to spend time ashore and to devote his energies, over a twelve-year period, to farming and managing the Barham Court estate. He also owned a London house at Hanover Square, where he could attend to his burgeoning naval career. He was a highly political animal, becoming Comptroller of the Navy in August 1778. He was awarded a baronetcy in 1781 and three years later was elected as MP for Rochester.

He introduced James Ramsey, whom he knew from his sailing days, to the circle of friends at Barham Court. Ramsay had served as ship's surgeon on board HMS *Arundel* when it was under the command of Charles Middleton. Later he gave up being a surgeon to become an Anglican vicar and worked tirelessly on the Caribbean island of St Kitts to improve working conditions for the plantation slaves. Margaret had been involved in correspondence with Ramsay over a twenty-year period. Now he was appointed secretary to Sir Charles Middleton, and given the living at Teston Church and made Rector at nearby Nettlestead.

Another visitor to the group came at the invitation of Ramsay – the indefatigable Thomas Clarkson, who became curate at Teston and went on to be a founder member of the Society for the Abolition of the Slave Trade. He was to devote his whole life to criss-crossing the country giving lectures, interviewing sailors and collecting signatures to his anti-slavery petitions.

Another guest was John Newton – a former slaver who had himself been reduced to servitude and abject poverty by a disgruntled slave trader on an island off the coast of Sierra Leone. When he eventually escaped and returned to Britain he experienced an epiphany when the ship he was on board nearly sank off the coast of Ireland. Eventually recanting of his old ways, he became a firebrand of a preacher and, among other things, went on to write the anti-slavery song 'Amazing Grace'.

In this way Barham Court became the place where all the threads of the anti-slavery movement came together. Friendships were forged, roles were worked out, and the leading lights went forth, imbued with determination to get the message across.

Ramsay had seen the appalling treatment of slaves first-hand during his time in the West Indies. What alarmed him was not just the cruelty but also the apparent indifference shown by people with whom he raised the topic. But with Margaret and her husband he found sympathetic listeners – they rebuilt his confidence, convincing him that he had a duty to speak out. They helped him draft what became an important treatise on slavery, which was published in 1784 as a book-length tract called an *Essay on the Treatment and Conversion of African Slaves in the British Sugar Colonies*. The preface to the tract was a lengthy letter which was in fact written by Margaret, Lady Middleton. Clarkson was to say of Ramsay's book that it was the 'first controversy ever entered into on the subject, during which, as is the case in most controversies, the cause of truth was spread'. It certainly helped light the fuse under the abolitionist cause, and inspired a generation of activists to campaign against the degrading and barbaric trade in human misery.

1788 saw the publication of another paper by Ramsay entitled *An Inquiry into the Effects of Putting a Stop to the African Slave Trade*. His works were extremely influential – he had seen the horrors of slavery at first hand, and he was a mainstream Anglican clergyman whose ideas could not be dismissed out of hand.

Ramsay's success, coupled with the generosity of the Middletons as hosts, and Sir Charles's increasing importance as a reformer of the Royal Navy, meant that influential visitors were eager to attend the Middleton dinner parties. In private meetings such as these the nascent abolition movement took hold. Strategies and tactics were discussed – and it was clear that a parliamentary voice was essential. Around this time the daughter of Charles and Margaret got married – and her husband had been at St John's College, Cambridge, with William Wilberforce. William was introduced to the regular gatherings at Barham Court, meeting Ramsay in 1783. He loved the Barham Court atmosphere, writing later that he found Barham Court 'in high preservation. It has none of the grand features of your northern beauties but for the charms of softness and elegance I never beheld a superior to Barham Court'.

In 1788 Charles Middleton addressed the House of Common on the evils of the slave trade, and his wife asked whether he was prepared to spearhead the abolition campaign in Parliament. He declined, saying that William Wilberforce 'not only displayed very superior talents of great eloquence, but was a decided and powerful advocate of the cause of truth and virtue'. In practice, it was a wise choice – Middleton remained to serve as a most effective Comptroller of the Navy, introducing much needed reforms, eradicating corruption and improving the lot of the common sailor, with increased pay and better conditions. He was eventually made up to Admiral (June 1795) and was appointed First Lord of the Admiralty (1805). When he retired from office he was given the title of Baron Barham of Teston. He died aged 86 on 17 June 1813.

And what of his wife Margaret? She died suddenly in 1792. The timing was significant because in that same year John Thornton purchased an estate in Clapham and it quickly took over from Barham Court as the centre of the abolitionist cause. The Clapham Sect carried on where the salons of Margaret, Lady Middleton had left off. But although she did not live to see her cause carried through to the statute book, she was hugely influential. In an era where it was not particularly fashionable to 'wear your heart on your sleeve' and promote your evangelical Christian beliefs, she relentlessly used her social clout and network of contacts to further her chosen cause. Faith and philanthropy were inseparable in her mind – a combination which was to find an echo in the life of Elizabeth Fry, featured in Chapter 16.

✳✳✳✳

Margaret was by no means the only female abolitionist, as borne out by Hannah More (see Chapter 15). Together she and Margaret had badgered the manager of the Drury Lane Theatre Royal to put on Thomas Southerne's adaptation of Aphra Behn's *Orrinooko*, as a way of getting the play's anti-slavery message across to thousands of theatregoers. As Hannah said in her letter to Margaret:

> *I know of no place but the play-house where three thousand people meet every night. Many people go to a play who never go to church, and if they do go to church few preachers except the Bishop of Chester and Mr Ramsay will vindicate the right of slaves.*

1788 was the centenary of the Glorious Revolution (which had put William of Orange on the English throne). Hannah marked the anniversary by publishing her poem, *Slavery*. It was intended to show the contrast between the country's self-image as the land of freedom, and the reality of the situation, i.e. of a country which systematically condemned Africans to enslavement. Hannah was also a friend (at least initially) of the Bristol milkwoman Ann Yearsley. Ann achieved a measure of fame as a writer of pro-abolition poetry but eventually the two women fell out over allegations of plagiarism. Another woman who wrote poems about the evils of the slave trade was Georgiana, Duchess of Devonshire; while in 1792 Mary Birkett Card had written *A Poem on the African Slave Trade*.

Quaker women were in the vanguard of the crusade, with supporters such as Anne Knight, who formed the Chelmsford Female Anti-Slavery Society, and much later on, the firebrand Elizabeth Hesketh. In 1824, she published her pamphlet 'Immediate not Gradual Abolition' and was particularly effective in the Birmingham area in gaining support for outright abolition of slavery. Her group, known as the 'Female Society for Birmingham', contributed significantly to central funds of the Anti-Slavery Society, and threatened to withdraw all support unless the Society took a more positive and immediate stance against slavery. She won the support of over seventy women's groups across the country, and it worked – the Anti-Slavery Society dropped the words 'gradual abolition' from its title.

Above all, when Josiah Wedgwood came up with the idea of a brooch featuring a slave in chains under the motto 'Am I not a man and a brother?' (with its alternative, 'Am I not a woman and a Sister?') it quickly became a fashion accessory worn blatantly and proudly by men and women alike as a badge of their belief.

In 1792 progress through Parliament of Bills opposing slavery had become bogged down. A brilliant and successful grassroots campaign was launched to boycott West

Indian sugar – to hit the plantation owners where it hurt most, i.e. in their pockets. This was perhaps the first time that consumer power had been tried. Housewives simply refused to buy sugar from the West Indies. They either went without – or followed the call to use sugar grown in plantations in the East Indies where slaves were not used as labour. Some 300,000 households adopted the boycott – and credit for that must go to the women in those households, since they were the ones who actually bought the food to be consumed by their families. The result has been estimated as a 30 per cent drop in consumption of Caribbean sugar, and manufacturers leapt on the bandwagon by producing sugar dispensers with the words 'East India Sugar – not made by Slaves'.

Margaret's gatherings around the dinner table differed from many of the other meetings arranged by the better-known *salonnières* such as Elizabeth Montagu and Elizabeth Vesey of the Blue Stockings Society, or the gatherings organised by Hester Thrale. For a start, Margaret's discussion groups were private – and they had just one topic for discussion. Other salons encompassed a far wider range of topics. Remember, this was the time of the loss of Britain's colonies in America, and of the French Revolution. Freedom of speech was a much-trumpeted right – and yet it sat uncomfortably with the laws on sedition, blasphemy, defamation and copyright. These topics raised big questions about Britain's role in the world, about the powers of the monarchy and the rights of the common man, and these questions were debated in the salons of the day. Many of which were open to men as well as women.

For women it gave a chance to listen – and be listened to. They had a voice, and a chance to influence others. Small wonder that the gatherings were derided by caricaturists – such as Thomas Rowlandson's *Breaking up the Blue Stocking Club* shown at Plate 9. Significantly, the hostess could dictate the topics to be discussed at each meeting, in order to make the discussions focussed. The arts and literature might be discussed at one meeting, science and metaphysical subjects at another. The Blue Stockings Society had started around 1750 and was intended to be a literary discussion group, a social and educational meeting where political topics were barred. In time a number of discussion groups, societies and debating clubs opened up in many parts of the country. Some were formed as special interest groups – for instance to promote the abolition of slavery. Others were simply designed for women to have an opportunity to socialise and discuss general topics of interest. Many had one thing in common – unlike the Blue Stockings Society they were not open to men.

Elizabeth Montagu, *salonnière*.

Plate 9

Elizabeth Raffald, holding her famous cook book.
See page 89

Breaking up the Blue Stocking Club illustrating the widespread (male) view that a largely female gathering would inevitably lead to furious arguments and that members would quickly come to blows. See page 107

Plate 10

Hannah More. See page 114

Plate 11

Mary Wollstonecraft – proto-feminist or immoral harridan? Painted hyena or an extraordinary visionary, a woman before her time? See page 122

Plate 12

Virgin shape Warehouse. Men tended to see women as being preoccupied with shopping, and with deceiving men by altering their shape...

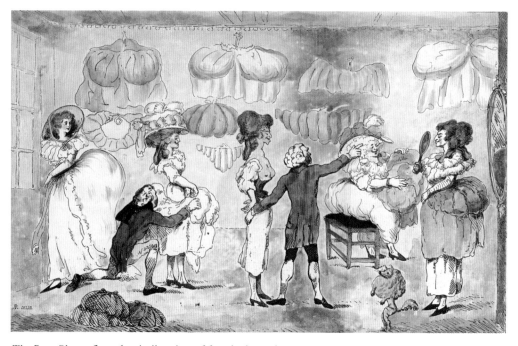

The Bum Shop reflected a similar view of female deception.

Plate 13

Six Stages of mending a face shows a woman's fondness for deceit in the way she puts on her wig, applies make-up and so on.

BILLINGSGATE BRUTES.

Billingsgate Brutes demonstrates the perception that women just stand around gossiping…

Plate 14

The Elopement echoes the view that all that girls wanted was to run off with a man in uniform....

Plate 15

The Boarding-School Hair-Drefser.   144

The Boarding School Hairdresser suggests a
view by men that Girls' Schools were hotbeds
of immorality and licentious behaviour.
Note the girl's legs locked round the
stylist's limbs…

Domestick Amusement: The Lovely Spinner.

Ah, the joys of spinning! *Domestick
amusement: The lovely spinner.*

Plate 16

… and the fun to be had from sewing a seam!
Domestick amusement: The fair seamstress.

…to say nothing of the pleasure to be
had from smoothing out those creases!
Domestick Employment – Ironing.

Chapter 15

Hannah More – bluestocking, educationalist and pamphleteer

Hannah More was born in Bristol on 2 February 1745, the fourth of five daughters whose father was a schoolmaster. He had originally hoped to pursue a career in the Church but, after losing a lawsuit over an estate he had hoped to inherit, he moved to Bristol and became an excise officer. Later he was appointed teacher at the Fishponds free school and Hannah grew up in a female-dominated environment, immersed in all directions by the world of education – first as a pupil, then later as a teacher.

Her father taught her mathematics, or at least, he did until she became too proficient and he feared that she was becoming too precocious for her own good. He also taught her Latin. Her elder sisters taught her French, and she became fully fluent after she was permitted to converse with French prisoners of war held in the encampment known as 'Frenchay' in Bristol during the Seven Years War. She was fiercely intelligent, an avid learner and something of an intellectual. She learned Italian, as well as Spanish, and from an early age wrote poetry and short stories.

When two of her elder sisters were sent by their father to start a boarding school for girls at 6 Trinity Street, Bristol, in 1758, Hannah went there as a pupil, stayed on, and became a teacher herself. Aged 22 she became engaged to a man called William Turner, a wealthy landowner twenty years her senior living at nearby Tyntesfield, in Somerset. It was presumably seen as a logical way of ensuring her financial independence – but the years dragged on without the marriage taking place. There are reports that he even got as far as the altar on one occasion, before having a change of mind. Quite why Turner was so reluctant to commit himself is unclear, but in 1773 the six-year deadlock was finally broken: the engagement was terminated and in return Turner agreed to pay Hannah an annuity of £200. Hannah may have been devastated – and apparently suffered a form of nervous breakdown at what must have been a humiliating and public rejection, but the money certainly helped. It gave her independence and a regular income, a solid foundation from which she could pursue her new chosen career – a life as a professional writer.

As a teenager she had already enjoyed literary success with her highly moralistic *Search after Happiness*, a play designed to be performed by young ladies at her school. By 1773 the play had been published in London and was a considerable success, selling upwards of 10,000 copies during the following ten years. A twelfth edition came out in 1800.

Various other plays and moralistic stories followed. In particular, *Essays on Various Subjects, Principally Designed for Young Ladies*, was published, anonymously in 1777. These eight essays looked at such topics as education and religion, and gave Hannah a chance to expound her views on the role of women in society. She fully accepted that men and women were different, and had different roles. She also accepted that the role of women was secondary to that of men, but maintained that education and a strict moral code were essential. Great attention should be paid to the intellectual, sentimental, and religious education of girls, and More described female conduct as 'one of the principal hinges on which the great machine of human society turns'.

For each of the next thirty-five years Hannah and two of her sisters would travel to London where Hannah swiftly established herself as one of the 'glitterati' – someone who mixed with the cream of London's intellectual writers and artists. Her circle quickly included the actor David Garrick, Dr Samuel Johnson, Sir Joshua Reynolds and Edmund Burke. She became a staple of the Blue Stocking literary salons, headed by Elizabeth Montagu in Hill Street and later in Portman Square, and by Elizabeth Vesey in Clarges Street, and by Frances Boscawen in South Audley Street. She had her portrait painted by popular artists, including Henry William Pickersgill (see Plate 14). Later, she was to commemorate the salon culture in her 1782 poem *The Bas Bleu, or, Conversation*, published in 1784. Dr Johnson appeared to take a particular shine to her, describing her as 'the finest versifatrix [in other words, female writer of verse] in the English language'. Garrick enthusiastically persuaded her to put on plays, first in Bath and later at Covent Garden. Her play *Percy*, first performed in December 1777, was a big hit with the critics and the theatre-going public alike, and Hannah made £600 from the copyright sales.

Her output became increasingly more evangelical, as she came to appreciate the power of drama in influencing behaviour and of informing and educating the audience. She wrote another play, called *The Fatal Falsehood*, which was produced in 1779, but it was a resounding flop and Hannah never wrote for the stage again. The failure may have tainted Hannah's addiction to the London literary scene – that, and the death of David Garrick in January 1779. There was also an unfortunate accusation by the poet Ann Yearsley that Hannah had misappropriated profits generated by Yearsley's *Poems, on Several Occasions* published in 1785. No matter that Hannah and Elizabeth Montagu had placed the money in a trust, thinking that this would protect Ann Yearsley from losing all the money to her profligate husband. Hannah was devastated at the accusation of theft, and quickly dropped out of her old circle of literary friends and headed back to Bristol to start the next stage in her life, as a moral crusader and philanthropist.

By then she had already developed a close friendship with luminaries such as the notorious gossip Horace Walpole, as well as the MP William Wilberforce. A more serious reflective tone appeared in her writings, with *Sacred Dramas* published in 1782, quickly running through nineteen editions. This was followed by *Thoughts on the Importance of the Manners of the Great to General Society* (1788), and *An Estimate of the Religion of the Fashionable World* (1790). She became a leading supporter of abolition, and published a poem entitled *Slavery* in 1788, becoming part of the Teston Set referred to in the preceding chapter. Margaret Middleton, Granville Sharp, James Ramsay and other leading abolitionists were all included in her circle of friends.

By the mid-1780s she had settled in the Somerset village of Wrington in a house at Cowslip Green, where she lived with her sister Martha. She started writing simple tracts, part prose, part verse, with a strong moral didactic tone. *Village Politics, by Will Chip* came out in 1792 and was intended as an antidote to the inflammatory works of Thomas Paine and reflected concerns about the risk of social unrest in the aftermath of the French Revolution. These simple tracts were then developed specifically for the rural poor, becoming a phenomenally popular series of penny broadsheets published as Cheap Repository Tracts between 1795 and 1797. They sold not just in thousands but in hundreds of thousands, and by 1797 an estimated two million copies were being bought and distributed among the rural poor of the nation. The success of these simple pamphlets led to the formation of the Religious Tract Society, founded in 1799.

The tone of the tracts was simple: live within your means, stay sober, read the Bible and respect your betters. The whole series, produced at the rate of two or three different tracts each month, was entirely pro-monarchy, pro-Church (and anti-French).

To that extent, Hannah More was a complete antithesis of Mary Wollstonecraft mentioned in Chapter 17. Hannah was no revolutionary, she was a supporter of the *status quo* in government – and indeed in the role of women. Hannah famously declined to read Wollstonecraft's *Rights of Women* saying: 'so many women are fond of government ... beacuse they are not fit for it. To be unstable and capricious is but too characteristic of our sex.'

Hannah's overriding interest was in educating women so that they could best perform their role – as wife, mother, and homemaker. Education formed the basis of her philanthropy. She started a school in Wrington and later extended this to a network of a dozen schools throughout the Mendip area, from Cheddar to Shipham, Blagdon, and Nailsea. In doing so she trod on a lot of toes, particularly the local Church of England vicars who saw her teachings as a threat and a criticism. Stirred up by opposition from the farming community (who were concerned that educating the females would make them dissatisfied with their lot, and become more demanding), local clergy started a vitriolic campaign against Hannah.

She persevered and became a highly respected philanthropist, using her reputation to inspire other women to follow her example. Doing 'good works' for the benefit of the poor became fashionable. In 1799 her *Strictures on the Modern System of Female Education* came out, in two volumes, and achieved a huge success, with seven editions coming out in the first year alone. It encapsulated all her views on the education of women, and their role in society. Education was essential because, as she says in the Introduction:

> *It is a singular injustice which is often exercised towards women, first to give them a very defective Education, and then to expect from them the most undeviating purity of conduct; to train them in such a manner as shall lay them open to the most dangerous faults, and then to censure them for not proving faultless.*

The *Strictures* set out the proposition that the 'chief end to be proposed in cultivating the understandings of women, is to qualify them for the practical purposes of life' – in other words: as wives and mothers. Hannah emphasised the role of women in maintaining a strict moral line – they were the influencers, whereas men were the doers. She expresses the view in the opening chapter of her book that there is one talent which 'women of the higher class have, the importance of which they can scarcely rate too highly. This talent is influence'.

Hannah maintained that a proper education enabled a woman to be a better housekeeper ('A sound economy is a sound understanding brought into action') and stressed that the type of education she advocated would prepare her, not for competition with men, but for an acceptance of her role ('The more her judgment is rectified, the more accurate views will she take of the station she was born to fill and the more readily will she accommodate herself to it'). Inflammatory it may be to today's ears, but it found favour in the Victorian era and helped foster the 'children, cooking and church' role for women, against which modern feminists rail.

In 1801 Hannah brought out her only novel, *Coelebs in Search of a Wife*, an idealised picture of a good husband and his subservient wife. She went on to outlive her sisters and died in Clifton, Bristol, on 7 September 1833 at the age of 88; a towering figure of the Georgian era and a hugely respected and successful author. She was buried alongside her sisters in the churchyard at All Saints' Church in Wrington. Her Will dealt with the administration of her estate, amounting to some £30,000, with the majority being left to religious societies and charitable organisations.

****

For such an orthodox, ultra-conservative person as Hannah More, it may seem odd to regard her as a paradigm-shifter. However, the very fact that she was a successful playwright, a poet, and an author of simple guides which influenced thousands of people, sets her apart from most of her contemporaries. Her ideas may seem old-fashioned nowadays, but they made perfect sense at the time, and she lived her life according to the rules which she laid down for others. She made being a professional writer respectable, and whereas her teaching may have fallen way short of the three Rs proposed by subsequent educationalists, at least she saw reading, and the dissemination of knowledge, particularly Christian knowledge, as having a value. Arguably she was a propagandist who provided 'the acceptable face of feminism' for the next 100 years. Small wonder then that she is now largely out of fashion – as if she is in some way to blame for 'not having gone far enough'. Perhaps the answer is that in a relay race, only the runner on the final leg crosses the finishing line – Hannah merely carried the baton on one of the earlier legs.

Hannah More, 1827.

Chapter 16

Elizabeth Fry – prison reformer

Elizabeth was born into a prominent Quaker family, the Gurneys of Norwich in 1780. Her father John was a merchant in charge of Gurney's bank, and mother Catherine was a scion of the Barclay banking family. They were respectable, middle class, and keen to educate their twelve children so that they could lead useful and fulfilled lives. Elizabeth, a nervous and often sickly child, was frequently absent from school and only learned to read and write at a comparatively late age. Her mother died at the age of 38 when Elizabeth was 12, and as one of the elder daughters it therefore fell to her to bring up the younger children in what was, by Quaker standards, a fairly lax household. Elizabeth stood apart from her siblings, especially once she was 18 and 'experienced the Lord' – earning her considerable derision from the rest of the family. She adopted the fiercely plain and austere dress of the devout Quaker, and lived her entire life in accordance with the strictest of Quaker ideals. Two years after her religious awakening she met and married Joseph Fry, grandson of Joseph and Anna Fry mentioned in Chapter 13. In the marriage certificate recording the wedding on 19 August 1800, young Joseph was described as a tea dealer. Given the family connections it is not surprising that in 1808 Joseph started his own bank. Elizabeth meanwhile was busy breeding: they had ten children by 1816, and an eleventh was born in 1822.

In 1809 Elizabeth, her husband, and her growing family had moved to Plashet House in East Ham. Here she was active in community work, feeding and clothing the poor of the parish, and encouraging vaccination against smallpox in an attempt to reduce the impact of this often fatal disease. She also helped found a small school for local children who would not otherwise have received an education.

In early 1813 the devout Elizabeth Fry made a tour of Newgate Prison to visit some of the 300 women incarcerated there. What she saw changed her life – and the lives of thousands of women throughout the following decades. There were two wards, and two separate cells, and into these the women were crammed, many with young children. In this confined space their whole daily life was lived – cooking, eating, sleeping and (to a very limited degree) washing. Conditions were squalid, filthy and depressingly stark. The inmates may have looked old beyond their years – the average age of female prisoners had dropped from around 37 in 1795 to just over 22 at the time of Elizabeth's visit. Many of them were still awaiting trial, and there was no segregation between murderers, shoplifters, or those charged with minor misdemeanours.

Touring the facilities Elizabeth remarked that: 'every thing was filthy to excess, and the smell was quite disgusting. Every one, even the Governor, was reluctant to go amongst them.' On another occasion she wrote: 'All I tell thee is a faint picture of reality; the filth, the closeness of the rooms, the furious manner and expressions of the women towards each other, and the abandoned wickedness, which everything bespoke are really indescribable.'

There were no beds – the women slept on the bare floor; their clothing was in tatters and as Elizabeth later noted, the women were 'pining away' for want of nourishment, fresh air and exercise. They had nothing to do in their free time except drink and gamble. One reporter noted that 'the language of indecency, violence, and blasphemy excited no surprise, for it was the common language of the place'. Even the youngest of the children would swear profanities as soon as they could learn to talk. The enormity of the problem facing Elizabeth is shown by looking at the somewhat tenuous link between crime, justice and punishment in the eighteenth century – and the even more remote connection between punishment and the compassionate treatment of offenders. Prisons were overcrowded, flea-ridden, disease-laden squalid dungeons. Elizabeth was horrified. Writing about what she saw as the reason for punishment she remarked: 'Punishment is not for revenge, but to lessen crime and reform the criminal.' That would have been news indeed for the inmates of some of the notorious prisons where people could be locked up for years on the strength of hearsay and malicious lies, after a trial lasting mere minutes and at which there would have been no counsel for the defence.

There were an extraordinary number of offences carrying the death penalty, many of them for what we would regard as minor offences involving the theft of property. Over the last sixty-five years of the eighteenth century some 1,600 women were given the death sentence in England and Wales, and the sentence was carried out in around 350 of those cases. The others were reprieved, with the sentence generally commuted to life imprisonment. A woman found guilty of murdering her husband was treated differently to a man killing his wife – such a crime went to the root of the master–servant relationship between spouses and hence was treated as Petty Treason. The significance of this is that women suffered a particularly excruciating death – being burned at the stake – right up until this barbaric form of execution was abolished in 1790. Felons found guilty of treason were dragged to the place of execution on the back of a hurdle or sled. If the poor woman was 'lucky' she would be garrotted by the executioner before the flames got under way, but there are instances where this failed and death would have been agonisingly slow. In the period 1735–90 there were thirty-two women burnt at the stake – either for Petty Treason or for High Treason (forging or counterfeiting the King's coinage). From 1790 High and Petty treason remained a capital offence, i.e. death by hanging, until the differentiation of the crime was abolished in 1828.

On execution days the men were usually hanged first, and the women would then be brought out in front of the men on the gallows to meet their fate. Age was no bar to being executed, and many of those hanged were teenagers. Most of the women sent to the gallows had been convicted of murder, nearly half of them for killing their illegitimate child. It gives some idea of the stigma attached to having a child out of wedlock, and of the near impossibility of a mother bringing up a child on her own without financial support. It was not until the Infanticide Act of 1922 that killing of a newborn child ceased to be a capital offence.

'Pleading your belly' (that is to say, claiming pregnancy) was a popular way of seeking to avoid the death penalty. For that reason, whereas men were generally led to the gallows within forty-eight hours of sentence being passed, women were given time to establish whether or not they were actually pregnant. Many would have turned to their male gaolers in a desperate attempt to get pregnant 'at all costs'. If they were successful, they and their future child would face years in prison.

After Britain lost the American War of Independence it was no longer possible to ship prisoners off to the American colonies, and the decision was made to transport felons to Australia. However, the ships making the journey were few and far between, and felons awaiting transportation, men and women, were incarcerated in rotting hulks – old warships moored up in the River Thames. Here the conditions were perhaps the most awful, with cholera and typhus rampant.

From the moment that a woman was arrested she would have been faced with appalling conditions. If she was arrested at night by the night watchman she would be thrown into one of the notorious watch-houses (each parish had one) where 'guests' were kept overnight until they could be examined by a Justice of the Peace in the morning. In 1724 four women suffocated to death in the watch-house known as St Martin's Roundhouse. They were among a group of several dozen disorderly women rounded up and thrown into the prison, the doors and windows tightly shut. In the morning four were found to have died, two died shortly afterwards and the others were in a terrible condition. None had been convicted of a crime and some may have been going about their business perfectly lawfully. They were simply in the wrong place at the wrong time, when some over-zealous official decided to round up vagabonds, prostitutes, streetwalkers and anyone else who just happened to be around that night. Perhaps surprisingly (perhaps not) the keeper William Bird was hauled before the Old Bailey and put on trial for murder. He was found guilty. It was one of many such instances which promoted a demand for change. Reports of extortion, cruelty and rape were commonplace.

What is surprising is the sheer number of places where prisoners could be incarcerated. Writing in the 1720s Daniel Defoe, in his *Tour thro' the Whole Island of Great Britain*, mentioned that there were twenty-two 'public gaols' and many more 'tolerated prisons' in London. Most of these were run on commercial lines, with the gaoler being paid in accordance with a scale of fees set by the Justices of the Peace. It was not uncommon for gaolers to supplement their income by charging prisoners for clothing, extra food and other 'privileges'. In particular, the Fleet prison (used entirely to house debtors) was known as being the biggest brothel in the whole of London.

In many respects prison inmates were left to look after themselves. Basically, the prison authorities locked them up and left them to their own devices, and it was not until Elizabeth Fry came along that the female prisoners received the help they needed to help themselves. She discussed her plans with the prisoners and got them to agree to organise a prison school. She introduced Bible classes and personally gave readings every Friday. She encouraged a team of women to help her improve conditions in gaol, recognising the power and importance of 'women working together for women'. Prison dress was introduced, and alcohol and gambling was banned. In April 1817 she formed the Ladies' Association for the Reformation of the Female Prisoners in Newgate, aiming:

> to provide for the clothing, the instruction, and the employment of these females, to introduce them to knowledge of the holy scriptures, and to form in them as much as lies in our power, those habits of order, sobriety, and industry which may render them docile and perceptible whilst in prison, and respectable when they leave it.

Four years later the scope of the group was extended to cover all women in all prisons, becoming known as the 'British Ladies' Society for Promoting the Reformation of Female Prisoners'. As such it can be regarded as the very first female organisation operating right across the whole of Britain.

In 1818 she became the first woman ever to give evidence to a parliamentary committee looking into prison conditions. Elizabeth's ideas transformed the prison environment. A place where society had dumped what were regarded as the vilest dregs of humanity became places of hope. Kindness replaced cruelty, and soon the fame of Elizabeth Fry spread nationwide, acquiring her the name 'the angel of prisons'.

Her success seems to have surprised even her, writing about the female prisoners in 1817: 'Already, from being like wild beasts, they appear harmless and kind.'

She travelled extensively around Britain, and later throughout the continent, addressing women's groups and pressing for further changes. Always, she urged the creation of local female committees to arrange prison visits. Elizabeth also campaigned against capital punishment, was opposed to solitary confinement for women, called for greater religious tolerance, and pressed for improvements in the conditions on board the prison ships heading for Tasmania and New South Wales.

Her book entitled *Observations on the Visiting, Superintendence, and Government, of Female Prisoners* came out in 1827 followed in 1840 by *Hints on the Advantages and the Duties of Ladies' Committees who Visit Prisons.* According to the Oxford Dictionary of National Biography she also 'established a Maternal Society in Brighton in 1813, libraries for the coastguard of England, several district visiting societies, a servant's society, and a Society of Nursing Sisters (1840), the first attempt to reform nursing in Britain'. Indeed, when a young Florence Nightingale first went to the Crimea she took with her a small group of Fry's nurses to help treat the wounded.

One other incident marks Elizabeth out as exceptional: in 1832 she was permitted access to observe a debate in the House of Commons. It is worth remembering that women had been banned from observing proceedings in the chamber of the House during the preceding fifty years. Matters had come to a head on 2 February 1778 when a large group of male protesters were ejected from the viewing gallery because of their unruly conduct during a debate on the war with America. Lord North shortly afterwards started to address the House. His wife, accompanied by a number of female friends, was in the public gallery when the decision was made to evict them, in case they emulated the male protesters. An unruly demonstration followed and thereafter women were barred from viewing proceedings altogether. Eventually rules were introduced allowing females in groups of eight to visit the chambers, but only if they had applied in advance for a visitor's ticket from a Member of Parliament. Males needed no such prior arrangement.

Later, after 1834 when the Palace of Westminster was damaged by fire, the decision was made to spend £400 on creating a tiny space in the roof void, described by some as being like the Black Hole of Calcutta, where upwards of twenty women could sit, peering down on proceedings through metal grilles. No wonder the space was known as the Ladies Cage and reputedly resembled an oriental harem!

The fact that Elizabeth was allowed to view proceedings, and that this led to albeit limited access to a ladies section of the Strangers Gallery, is a measure of the respect in which she was held. Previously, Members had taken the view that women were a distraction; they might hear and see things which would 'not at all times be agreeable to their feelings'; it would be 'inconvenient, and destructive of that delicacy of the female character' and besides, men needed a sanctuary where they could escape from female censure. Indeed, when a proposal was made to allow a measure of ventilation in the 'Ladies Cage' and that money should be spent on modifying the partitioning, the Earl of Lincoln opposed the measure on the grounds that it had been suggested to the House as 'a mere joke' and should not be treated seriously. The improvements were not made until after 1864 – nearly 100 years after women had been barred altogether.

Elizabeth Fry suffered a stroke and died in Ramsgate in 1845. She was buried at the Society of Friends Burial Ground in Barking, Essex, and her achievements have subsequently been recognised on postage stamps, bank notes, memorials and numerous statues. Many of her ideas later became unfashionable and were overtaken by the ideas of male prison reformers, but she was an inspiration in her lifetime, because she refused to accept that nothing could be done to help those in greatest need.

****

In the first half of the century there was little attempt to segregate prisoners, either according to gender or according to whether they were felons or merely debtors who had committed no criminal act. Worse, there was inadequate or non-existent medical supervision, and disease was rampant. In one outbreak of typhus in 1750 the infection spread from the prison to the courtroom, killing the Lord Mayor of London along with Sir Thomas Abney, judge of the Common-Pleas, the under sheriff, some of the counsel, several of the jury, and another fifty or so other court officials, dignitaries and dogsbodies.

Overcrowding lay at the heart of the problem with the prisons – coupled with an apparent indifference as to how prisoners were treated, and a lack of concerted opinion as to what should be the objective of long term imprisonment. It was no coincidence that when the Gordon Riots occurred in London in 1780 the rioters made a point of attacking the prisons and houses of correction. Eight were destroyed, including the notorious Clink as well as Newgate, the Fleet, New Prison, King's Bench Prison, the Borough Compter and the Clerkenwell and Surrey Houses of Correction. The destruction merely added to the congestion in the already overcrowded gaols, and in time all were rebuilt but without modernisation or significant improvement (apart from the Clink, which remained as a ruined shell until it was eventually pulled down). Various parliamentary reports into the state of the prisons had been commissioned. In the 1770s books appeared in which the objective of reforming the criminal was put forward, such as Cesare Beccaria's *Of Crimes and Punishments*, translated into English in 1767. An emphasis on hard labour, but linked with religious instruction, was put forward for debate.

Meanwhile new designs for prisons were promulgated, where the more notorious criminals could be kept under constant supervision, such as with Jeremy Bentham's idea for a panopticon – a design for rows of cells radiating out from a central hub like the spokes of a bicycle wheel. Bentham intended it as the design for a national penitentiary, to be built at Millbank. The central hub was designed to enable the guard, via mirrors, to keep every single one of the prisoners under surveillance, without being detected. It was never actually implemented, although a somewhat similar design for a circular prison was constructed in Cuba in the 1920s. Some features of the panopticon were incorporated into the design for Pentonville when it was built in 1842. Other somewhat similar design ideas were implemented, such as at Coldbath Fields where wings of individual cells radiated out from a central vaulted courtyard.

One alternative attempt at reducing overcrowding was the simple expedient of releasing large numbers of people whose only crime was to be unable to pay their bills. Debtors accounted for the great majority of people in prison, and between 1700 and 1800 there were thirty-two Insolvency Acts passed, designed to free-up space in prisons such as the Fleet.

It became fashionable for philanthropic gentlemen such as Jonas Hanway and John Howard to visit prisons and submit proposals for reform. Howard was especially influential, and for that reason is remembered today in the name of the Howard League for Penal Reform. In 1777 John Howard condemned the disorganised, barbaric and filthy conditions in London's prisons and demanded immediate improvements. Some calls produced results, as in the Health of Prisoners Act of 1774, which established that each prison should have separate infirmaries for men and women, and that each prison should have a nominated apothecary and surgeon. In 1784 legislation was passed requiring a system of regular inspections of county gaols to be put in place, and putting an end to liquor and gambling being permitted. By the time a new prison-building programme got under way in the 1790s, with new prisons being built such as the Giltspur Street Compter and the Horsemonger Lane Gaol, prisoners were segregated according to the nature of their crime as well as according to their gender. Hard labour (such as dredging the Thames, or working in the docks) and solitary confinement were also introduced, in the firm belief that side-by-side, these two punishments would give the felon a chance to contemplate the folly of his ways, and turn to God for redemption. It is unlikely that many of the prisoners saw it that way…

Under lock and key.

Chapter 17

Mary Wollstonecraft – feminist and writer

If Hannah More was the acceptable face of a movement to promote the rights of women, Mary Wollstonecraft was the face which was both unacceptable and abhorrent. Hers was a life so extraordinary and unconventional that people were so horrified when they found out about it – about the attempted suicides, the depression, the illegitimate child, the wanton and reckless behaviour – that her message became clouded by the story of her life. Victorian moralists were so appalled by her actions that they dismissed her writings as evidence of her own depraved existence. If anything, she was held up as an anti-role model (i.e. this is what happens to you if you follow this set of beliefs).

It would be unfair to call her a feminist since the word was not identified in the English language, according to the Oxford English Dictionary, until 1852. In time the feminist movement emerged, to be associated with the call for female emancipation. But what Mary was advocating was perhaps far more radical – equal rights for women not just in the polling booth and in marriage but in education, in business opportunities, and in power.

If she cannot be called a feminist, or a proto-feminist, what was she called? According to Horace Walpole she was a 'painted hyena', while her own husband conceded that she had a 'rigid, and somewhat amazonian temper'. She herself was aware that her life choices were somewhat singular, writing to her sister Everina in November 1787, 'I am … going to be the first of a new genus. You know I am not born to tread in the beaten track — the peculiar bent of my nature pushes me on.'

So, what were the facts of her life? Born in London's Spitalfields in 1759, into a family presided over by an alcoholic father who became increasingly violent as the family fortunes declined, she found herself frequently uprooted. Her mother was weak and unsympathetic, and it must have been an unsettled childhood as the family moved around the country – to Epping, to Yorkshire, back to Hoxton in London, and then to Wales. She finally left home at the age of 18, poorly educated, and secured a job as a lady's companion to an irascible woman in Bath.

Convinced of the importance of giving girls a proper education, she returned to London in 1784 and started a school for girls in Newington Green. The school failed, and Mary then travelled to Ireland for a couple of years, working as a governess.

By the time she returned to settle in London in 1787 she had already had published a short tract entitled 'Thoughts on the Education of Daughters'. This conduct book, typical of many aimed at middle-class households, was not a great commercial success, but it was well reviewed in some quarters. Nowadays we might dismiss her arguments that a good education was necessary in order to enable a woman to be a good wife and mother – in other words to be a success in the domestic sphere – as being far too reactionary. But this was an early work, and contained ideas which only really took flight after the start of the apocalyptic revolution in France, which suddenly opened Mary's mind to far more important things than female education *per se*.

On the other hand, it included an interesting analysis of her own place in society, particularly in a chapter entitled 'Unfortunate Situation of Females, Fashionably Educated, and Left without a Fortune'. Here she writes about being a lady's companion:

> *It is impossible to enumerate the many hours of anguish such a person must spend. Above the servants, yet considered by them as a spy, and ever reminded of her inferiority when in conversation with the superiors. … A teacher at a school is only a kind of upper servant, who has more work than the menial ones. A governess to young ladies is equally disagreeable. …life glides away, and the spirits with it; 'and when youth and genial years are flown,' they have nothing to subsist on; or, perhaps, on some extraordinary occasion, some small allowance may be made for them, which is thought a great charity…*

The book was published by Joseph Johnson and in 1787 Mary started her fourth job, as a translator, reader, reviewer, and editorial assistant for the *Analytical Review*, which was published jointly by Joseph Johnson and Thomas Christie. It was a brave step, embarking on an independent career as a female writer, and not one which many had tried before. Most significantly, the new job brought her into contact with progressive thinkers and radical new ideas, ideas which would shortly cause a veritable tsunami in the form of the French Revolution. Johnson, in particular, took Mary under his wing – he had advanced money to her against the publication of her book (an unheard of piece of generosity towards an unknown and unpublished author); had found lodgings for her; and included her in his regular 'Johnson Dinners' to which all the radical thinkers of the day were invited. Johnson was her friend and her father figure. Once, after a disagreement, she was to write to him:

> *You made me very low-spirited last night, by your manner of talking. You are my only friend—the only person I am intimate with. I never had a father, or a brother. You*

have been both to me, ever since I knew you—yet I have sometimes been very petulant. I have been thinking of those instances of ill-humour and quickness, and they appeared like crimes. Yours sincerely, Mary.

The storming of the Bastille on 14 July 1789 was not an isolated movement but an explosion born out of frustration at a society dominated by the aristocracy. The call for 'Liberty, Equality and Fraternity' was enthusiastically seized upon by radicals on both sides of the Channel and gave impetus for a movement based on overthrowing the old order and introducing democracy. In its early days, before the Terror turned many of its supporters against the Revolution, the overthrow of the French monarchy was seen as a wonderful, liberating, act. No wonder the British establishment recoiled in horror, as it feared that the flames of revolution would cross the Channel and threaten the Hanoverian throne. But it was not just political democracy which was being unleashed – it was a world of new ideas and new freedoms. Writing later, Mary drew a parallel between inequality within marriage with the inequality of the monarchy: 'The divine right of husbands, like the divine right of kings, may, it is hoped, in this enlightened age, be contested without danger.'

One of the first people to attack the Revolution and its supporters was Edmund Burke in his *Reflections on the Revolution in France.* Mary read it and immediately rattled off a pamphlet entitled *A Vindication of the Rights of Men*, defending the Revolution and its principles. This was published in 1790, bringing her into the public eye. She shared the same publisher as Tom Paine, who wrote the classic *The Rights of Man* in two parts in 1791. It was an extraordinary and successful analysis of the situation in France, calling for an end to hereditary government and for the introduction of a republican state, based upon social welfare. Later, Paine was tried in his absence for seditious libel against the Crown, found guilty, and sentenced to be hanged. Wisely, Paine remained in France and never made himself available for the sentence to be carried out. It did however show the dangers of expressing republican ideas; by the end of the decade Johnson too was to be hauled before the courts, found guilty of seditious treason, and carted off to prison for six months.

This was the background to Mary's response to events when, in 1792, she brought out her book entitled *A Vindication of the Rights of Woman.* The work was soon translated into French as well as being published in America and quickly made her famous, perhaps notorious, not just in England, but also throughout much of the Western world.

The *Vindication of the Rights of Woman* was far more than a political treatise, it was also an analysis of the role of women, the rationality of women, and the importance of the power of reasoning. Whereas Rousseau had argued that women were weak and not capable of employing reason, she responded by using reason to demolish those arguments. To her, men and women were equal in the eyes of God. Equally, both genders differed from animals because men and women could recognise truth and the difference between right and wrong – because they were rational human beings and were capable of exercising reason.

She saw no reason why men should have control over women, writing: 'If women be educated for dependence; that is, to act according to the will of another fallible being, and submit, right or wrong, to power, where are we to stop?'

She wanted female politicians, writing: 'Women ought to have representatives, instead of being arbitrarily governed without any direct share allowed them in the deliberations of government.'

Above all she wanted women to throw off the yoke of 'sensibility' – the idea that women were guided by their emotions and should worry at all times about appearances. To her:

Women are systematically degraded by receiving the trivial attentions which men think it manly to pay to the sex, when, in fact, men are insultingly supporting their own superiority.

On another occasion she wrote:

How many women thus waste life away … who might have practised as physicians, regulated a farm, managed a shop, and stood erect, supported by their own industry, instead of hanging their heads surcharged with the dew of sensibility, that consumes the beauty to which it at first gave lustre.

In calling for a full role for women in society, Mary was not denying their importance in the domestic sphere as mothers. As she said, 'Speaking of women at large, their first duty is to themselves as rational creatures, and the next, in point of importance, as citizens, is that … of a mother.'

Female education lay at the root of what Mary was calling for, arguing that only by educating women could society see what they were capable of achieving: 'Let their faculties have room to unfold, and their virtues to gain strength, and then determine where the whole sex must stand in the intellectual scale.' Hers was a call for empowerment, intellectual empowerment: 'Strengthen the female mind by enlarging it, and there will be an end to blind obedience.'

Mary was not just arguing that both sexes should have an equal education, she was at the vanguard of a call for co-education, i.e. with both genders being taught in the same classrooms, at the same time, so that they would share the learning experience.

While immersing herself in new and radical ideas Mary started to pursue a relationship with the artist Henry Fuseli. He was already married but, undeterred by this, Mary proposed that she move in with Henry and his wife. Even a 'platonic threesome' was not to the liking of Mrs Fuseli, who was horrified at the prospect. Mary may have been enraptured by Henry, writing of 'the grandeur of his soul, that quickness of comprehension, and lovely sympathy', but Henry was loyal to his wife and sent Mary packing.

If Mary's life had ended then, she would still have been a divisive figure, lauded by her followers and condemned and vilified by those who advocated the *status quo*. But that would have been all – she would have been judged on her writings. However, in December 1792 the peculiar bent of her nature did indeed push her off the beaten track – and caused her to move to Paris to be more involved in the changes brought about by the Revolution. In part, it may have been designed to take her away from the humiliation by Fuseli. From there her life took extraordinary twist after extraordinary twist. She soon met an American businessman, chancer, and opportunist called Gilbert Imlay. Her much vaunted 'reason' did not stop her falling in love with Imlay and by April 1793 they were involved in a passionate affair. Her staunch stand against conformity did not stop her recording her name as Gilbert Imlay's wife at the American Embassy – a deception which may dismay women nowadays, but which at the time seemed a sensible way of ensuring her personal safety, given that war with England was imminent and that being English, in France, was not a virtue to be proud of. By May 1794 Mary had given birth to a daughter. She called the girl Fanny, but by then Imlay's ardour had cooled and he disappeared off to London (and found himself a new partner). Mary, with baby in tow, was simply abandoned in Le Havre. Distraught, and suffering from depression which affected her on and off throughout her adult life, she waited in vain for Imlay to return. Describing her depression and her erratic and seemingly wayward behaviour, she was to write:

I am a strange compound of weakness and resolution! However, if I must suffer, I will endeavour to suffer in silence. There is certainly a great defect in my mind – my wayward heart creates its own misery. Why I am made thus I cannot tell; and, till I can form some idea of the whole of my existence, I must be content to weep and dance like a child, long for a toy, and be tired of it as soon as I get it.

December 1794 saw the publication in London of Mary's *An Historical and Moral View of the Origin and Progress of the French Revolution*. By April she had decided to follow Imlay to London. Here, for the first time, she discovered his deception and went to pieces.

Confronted by Imlay's decision to break off their affair, Mary twice tried to commit suicide. The first occasion seems to have been an attempt to take an overdose of laudanum, but she was prevented from doing so by Imlay. On the second occasion she jumped off Putney Bridge only to be saved by strangers. She had intended Imlay to read her suicide note after her death – it read:

Let my wrongs sleep with me! Soon, very soon, I shall be at peace. When you receive this, my burning head will be cold ... I shall plunge into the Thames where there is least chance of my being snatched from the death I seek. God bless you! May you never know by experience what you have made me endure. Should your sensibility ever awake, remorse will find its way to your heart; and, in the midst of business and sensual pleasure, I shall appear before you, the victim of your deviation from rectitude.

In between suicide attempts she had tried to ingratiate herself with Imlay by embarking on a hazardous Scandinavian tour to protect his business interests – with the infant Fanny in tow. She ended up publishing the story of her Nordic travels in January 1796 under the title of 'Letters Written During a Short Residence in Sweden, Norway and Denmark'.

By March 1796 Mary recognised the finality of the end of the relationship, and within a month had embarked on another adventure, this time renewing the acquaintance of one of the talking heads she had met in her days working for Johnson. The man, a notorious anarchist and political philosopher called William Godwin, was every bit a match for the ardent supporter of female empowerment. They fell in love, and she quickly became pregnant again. Around this time Mary started (but never finished) writing *Maria: or, The Wrongs of Woman*, a novelised version of her *Vindication* in which she describes the plight of a woman who is imprisoned in an asylum for the insane by her husband. It is a novel about injustice, and about female lack of power. As Mary says in the Preface:

In many instances I could have made the incidents more dramatic, would I have sacrificed my main object, the desire of exhibiting the misery and oppression, peculiar to women, that arise out of the partial laws and customs of society.

The novel was only to see the light of day, as a posthumous publication, in 1798.

William Godwin had described marriage as 'a monopoly – and the worst of monopolies' and had advocated the abolition of marriage in his treatise *'Political Justice'*, which had been published in 1793. Nevertheless, on 29 March 1797, the pair got married at St Pancras Church in London. They then moved into adjoining houses so that they could each retain their independence. This 'his and hers' arrangement may sound unorthodox, but it worked for them and they frequently communicated by letter. On 30 August 1797, Wollstonecraft gave birth to their daughter, Mary Wollstonecraft Godwin. Sadly, Mary only ever saw the first eleven days of her daughter's life – she suffered complications associated with an infection of the placenta and died on 10 September 1787. Her daughter eventually married the poet Percy Bysshe Shelley, after becoming pregnant, and, under her married name of Mary Shelley, became famous as the author of *Frankenstein*.

William Godwin published a biography of his wife Mary entitled *Memoirs of the Author of A Vindication of the Rights of Woman*, the year after her death. For the very first time the public were acquainted with the fact that Mary had never married Imlay. Her husband's openness about her affair, about the illegitimate Fanny, about the failed suicide attempts, may have been intended to show Mary in a more human light, but in practice it destroyed her reputation. Typical of the response to the lurid details of her life and death was the publication in 1798 of a poem by Richard Polwele entitled *The Unsex'd Females*. The polemic sought to link the excesses of the democracy movement and the revolution in France to the personal 'lustful conduct' of Mary Wollstonecraft. Her death was an example of the perils of succumbing to 'licentious love' Its author commented:

> *I cannot but think, that the Hand of Providence is visible, in her life, her death… As she was given up to her 'heart's lusts,' and let 'to follow her own imaginations', that the fallacy of her doctrines and the effects of an irreligious conduct, might be manifested to the world; and as she died a death that strongly marked the distinction of the sexes, by pointing out the destiny of women, and the diseases to which they are liable.*

In other words, she got what she deserved….

It would be a whole century before people started to look behind the 'shame and the scandal' and to see Mary's true legacy – her written works. They show a passion, a freedom of thought, and above all a rational response to what she perceived as the wrongs in society. Did she break paradigms? Yes, but only in the sense that, having blown them to pieces, all the bits fell back into exactly the same place. She defied convention, but did so in such a shocking way that few others would dare to follow. Her portrait is shown in Plate 11.

VINDICATION

OF THE

RIGHTS OF WOMAN:

BY MARY WOLLSTONECRAFT.

Conclusion

So, what are the conclusions to be drawn from these examples? How was it that some of these pioneers, having demolished the barriers, were unable to see their successes followed up by others? Or were women there all along, but we are no longer able to see them and to appreciate their significance?

To some extent the answer is that there have always been successful women, but that they have become invisible. It is easy to remember the Reynolds's, the Gainsbrough's and the Lawrence's – and then to forget that there was also Angelica Kauffmann, Maria Cosway and Elizabeth Leveson-Gower (the Duchess of Sutherland). We remember the great Shakespearean actor David Garrick – and perhaps add in Sarah Siddons alongside him – but forget that in the Georgian era, theatregoers would have been just as enthusiastic about Kitty Clive, Lavinia Fenton and Susannah Cibber. Conversely, just because twenty-first century tastes have promoted the works of Jane Austen into the stratosphere does not alter the fact that in her own lifetime Jane Austen was almost unknown. She never published a single title under her own name. Georgian readers would have been familiar with Fanny Burney, Eliza Haywood and Maria Edgworth. We now easily overlook Hannah Cowley, who wrote plays such as *The Runaway* and *The Belle's Stratagem* – plays which revolve around contemporary views of marriage and how women had to fight to overcome the straightjacket forced on them by family life and social custom. Elizabeth Inchbald is readily forgotten, even though she wrote no fewer than fifteen plays between 1785 and 1794, and all bar one were either published or put on the London stage.

Martha Gurney, Harriet Martineau and Ann Yearsley are no longer household names in the abolition movement but in their own time their writings were significant and effective. It is easy to forget that female preachers, especially in the Quaker movement, but also to some extent with the Methodists, were articulate in expressing moral outrage at the cruelty and injustices of the time. Margaret Fell who died in 1702 and was the wife of George Fox, helped found the Society of Friends, and way back in 1666 had written the influential pamphlet, *Women's Speaking Justified*, using the Scriptures to argue for a women's ministry. She argued passionately that God created all human beings, therefore both men and women were equal and both were capable of being a prophet and of possessing 'the Inner Light'. When Methodism started to spread in the 1730s female preachers were tolerated, and by the mid-1760s Sarah Crosby and Mary Bosanquet-Fletcher appeared to have set a precedent for female preaching. However, after John Wesley's death in 1791 male toleration of female preaching turned to outright opposition – from 1803 women were effectively permitted solely to address women-only assemblies. It was to be another 100 years before the situation was reversed in the Methodist movement– and the Church of England did not follow until after the Second World War.

Without prompting, it is easy to assume that there were no female architects – and yet it is now suggested that Elizabeth Wilbraham, who died in 1705, may have designed some 400 buildings, including eighteen churches normally credited to her pupil Christopher Wren. In science most credit is given to William Herschel – quite correctly – but it is unfair not to remember his sister Caroline Herschel who, after all, discovered eight comets. Thanks to her, women started to make strides towards acceptance in the world of science, but despite being the first female scientist to receive a pension from the State, and despite being awarded a gold medal by Royal Astronomical Society and becoming an honorary member of that body in 1835, her achievements are largely subsumed within the wider reputation of her illustrious brother. For some reason her achievements did not inspire others to follow in her wake – and that cannot have been entirely because of the anti-social nature of her working hours (i.e. at night) since that was equally trying for both men and women.

It is interesting to look at the people considered to be influential by critics at the time. In 1834 a book was published under the title of *The Georgian Era*, with four volumes listing those who were regarded as being the most eminent people to have flourished during the years 1714–1830. It contains profiles of some 1,800 men and (a few, a very few) women. Only three of the women profiled in this book got a mention (Hannah More, Anne Damer and Sarah Siddons). None of the rest were considered worthy of note, and certainly not Mary Wollstonecraft. She had perhaps shot herself in the foot by her unorthodox lifestyle and scandalous behaviour – her works nowadays may be considered an important milestone, but at the time they were dismissed out of hand as being the subversive ramblings of a deeply immoral woman. Others profiled here were regarded as appendages to their husbands (Margaret Middleton and Jane Marcet are cases in point). The rest were simply not 'eminent' – but then again, neither was Jane Austen!

In part, it may simply be a case of men just refusing to give credit to women for their achievements. As one female commentator of the time drily remarked 'whatever a man did was work, and what a woman did was her duty'. It was also a time when men were muscling in on the few areas which had traditionally been female orientated.

In some cases women did nothing to push back the boundaries because they simply resorted to deception in order to overcome prejudice – but in doing so did nothing to end that prejudice. Examples appear particularly in the armed forces. In the army, Phoebe Hessel is remembered for having disguised herself as a man in order to be able to accompany her soldier-lover, Samuel Golding, when he was posted to the West Indies. Her deception was eventually discovered when 'he' was ordered to be stripped to the waist so that 'he' could be whipped for misconduct. At that point she reputedly commented 'Strike and be damned!' Intriguingly the British Army allowed her to continue on full pay and many years later she was paid a pension by George IV and invited to attend his coronation procession in Brighton, where she ended her days at the age of 108.

To some extent it may have been ego on the part of the male businessmen ('Look at how successful I am – my wife doesn't have to work'), and women too may have revelled in this image and in the freedom it gave them to do other things. To Daniel Defoe, it was in part a case that the successful tradesman did not want his wife to be seen to work: '... he will have her sit above in the parlour, and receive visits, and drink tea, and entertain her neighbours, or take a coach and go abroad; but as to the business, she shall not stoop to touch it; he has apprentices and journeymen, and there is no need of it'.

Defoe famously remarked that women 'scorn to be seen in the counting house, much less behind the counter', and this suggests that women saw it as a sign of status that they were not required to work. And if a woman did engage in trade it might often be in order to protect the family business until it could be taken over by an infant son. As Defoe wrote in his *Complete English Tradesman:*

> *women, generally speaking ... act as if they were ashamed of being tradesmen's wives, and never intended to be tradesmen's widows. Thus I have known many a widow that would have thought it otherwise below her, has engaged herself in her husband's business, and carried it on, purely to bring her eldest son up to it, and has preserved it for him, and which has been an estate to him, whereas otherwise it must have been lost, and he would have had the world to seek for a new business.*

Defoe also singled out certain trades as being unsuited to females:

> *such as linen and woollen drapers, mercers, booksellers, goldsmiths, and all sorts of dealers by commission, and the like – custom, I say, has made these trades so effectually shut out the women, that, what with custom, and the women's generally thinking it below them, we never, or rarely, see any women in those shops or warehouses.*

That was a somewhat sweeping statement as shown by the number of trade cards for female mercers and drapers and so on, but it helps show that the attitude that 'it's not the done thing' was gaining strength. By the nineteenth century this had grown into a full-blown acceptance that 'a woman's place was in the home'. Queen Victoria was happy to be portrayed as 'the Mother of the Nation' and epitomised prevailing ideas on feminism and the importance of the family, motherhood and respectability.

There are other areas where the role of women has simply been downplayed. For instance, in the brewing trade it has been suggested that nearly three quarters of all brewsters were women, and yet with the hindsight of history we might assume that this was a trade dominated by men. Take an 'obviously male' occupation such as prison warden: it has been observed that between 1685 and 1775, one quarter of all jail keepers were female (probably having inherited the role on the death of the husband). Women were prominent throughout the country in the print business, with the indefatigable Mary Say being a case in point. She may have inherited a large printing company, but after her husband died she continued running it successfully throughout the last quarter of the century, and had a reputation for being a formidable businesswoman. However, because most of her contemporaries were men, she disappears from sight almost completely.

Whether or not a woman was married – and therefore whether or not she was affected by coverture – was of critical importance. Would the achievements of Hannah More, or Eleanor Coade have come about if they had been married? Probably not – or, if they had been married, their success would have been attributed to their husbands. Marriage provided a real Catch 22 situation. For a woman, faced with minimal employment opportunities, marriage was often the only financial security available. As Jane Austen said in a letter to her niece: 'Single women have a dreadful propensity for being poor, which is one very strong argument in favour of matrimony.' Women needed to marry if they were to lead financially secure lives – and yet the very fact of being married took away their freedom. This conflicting situation was brought about largely by the lack of education for girls, leading in turn to fewer employment opportunities in adulthood.

For the lower echelons of society, it can be argued that marriage was of little importance – unions either lasted, or they didn't, and if they didn't, there was no question of getting a divorce. However, for anyone with money, marriage was of critical importance. For a man who was not the eldest son, a marriage to a wealthy woman was likely to be his best chance of gaining a fortune. For a woman, unless she already had money, she was likely to be dependent on the charity of male members of her family for as long as she remained single. This was certainly the case with Jane Austen. Another female writer who was an exception which proved the point was Anna Seward, the Sapphic poet known as The Swan of Litchfield. She never married, but after her mother died she, in effect, took over the running of her father's household, became financially independent, and inherited her father's estate when he died. In a similar vein, Hannah More was able to escape the clutches of matrimony largely because she was 'paid off' by her erstwhile admirer.

Marriage worked for women, and it also worked against. For the Teresia Phillips's of this world, marriage was a device to be exploited, something to be used to cheat the system. For the unfortunate Mary Eleanor Bowes, mentioned on page xiii, conned into marriage by an Irish shyster, marriage was a hideous travesty of a loving relationship, and was simply a form of financial theft endorsed by the law.

Coverture may not always have been rigidly followed – some husbands may well have been happy to see their wives lead happy and fulfilled lives, and to give them credit for their commercial and artistic endeavours. But only if that suited the husband – and for many, coverture was like an invisibility cloak, because it served to hide the wife's achievements.

In many cases the woman was happy simply to be the power behind the throne. Sarah, the wife of Josiah Wedgwood, was a case in point. Known as Sally, she bought a substantial dowry into the marriage, and subsequently brought into the relationship an even greater inheritance when her brother died. Josiah was able to use this financial windfall to promote his new business venture at Eturia. But Sally was far more than the family banker – she was a shrewd operator, and better educated than her husband. She could see that his physical handicap (he eventually had to have one leg amputated because of a childhood illness) meant that his success rested not on the potter's wheel, which he could no longer operate, but as a man of business, as a pioneer of marketing techniques. She learnt the formulae, she observed the experiments, she kept the notes and records, and gave advice on shapes, colour and decoration. Josiah was not ungracious in admitting his indebtedness to Sally, writing to his friend Lord Gower:

> *I never had a great plan that I did not submit to my wife. She knew all the details of the business, and it was her love for the beautiful that first prompted and inspired me to take up Grecian and Roman Art, and in degree, reproduce the Classic for the world. I worked for her approval, and without her high faith in me I realize that my physical misfortunes would have overcome my will, and failure would have been written large where now England has carved the word Success.*

No doubt a similar debt of gratitude was owed by many other of the Georgian giants towards their wives, but it is interesting that in general, the women of the time were happy to step back and let their husbands take the limelight. Thus they remained invisible, and it makes it all the harder to assess their contribution.

The significance of the role played by leading Quakers has perhaps been overlooked because, as their nickname name suggests, they were derided and dismissed as religious zealots. However, the role of the members of the Society of Friends should not be forgotten, since their influence in trade and commerce has been enormous, out of all proportion to their numerical significance. Think Lloyds Bank and Barclays Bank, both founded by Quakers. Think of Friends Provident – the name rather gives its origins away, and until 1915 membership and policy-holding was only available to adherents of the Quaker faith.

Quakers have established an impressive roll call of household business names. The Quaker firm of C & J Clark started making shoes in 1825 when tanner James Clark made his first pair of leather slippers, known as Brown Petersburgs, by stitching together off-cuts from sheepskin fleeces being used to make rugs. Quickly spotting the potential, the company set up a network of homeworkers who would be given the suede blanks which would then be stitched up and made into completed slippers. The company, known as Clarks shoes, is still family controlled. Its longevity may in part be attributed to the fact that Quakers were generally less inclined towards primogeniture – on a death the estate was more likely to be shared equally between the children, regardless of gender, making for a broadly based family concern in which everyone has a say.

Another entrepreneurial Quaker was Robert Ransome, son of a schoolmaster, who went into the metal foundry business making cast-iron roofing plates. He discovered a system for casting self-sharpening ploughshares, and suddenly it was no longer necessary to re-sharpen the old-style wrought iron blades which blunted easily in the fields. He progressed to making detachable blades, cutting down still further the amount of time taken to repair ploughs. It was therefore a natural progression when Edwin Beard Budding came up with an invention to cut grass – the cylindrical lawn mower – and Ransomes started making them under licence in 1832.

The iron and steel industry owed its origins to the Quaker, Abraham Darby – the first of the Darbys of Coalbrookdale. He invented a process for making pig iron in a blast furnace heated not by charcoal, but by coke. His family expanded the business into making pots and pans, developing a virtual monopoly in these products. The Darby family business expanded, generally taking into partnership other Quakers such as Thomas Baylies (important because they had similar business values) and using finance from Quaker families, such as the Goldneys of Bristol. The first railway line in the country was installed between Stockton and Darlington, opening in 1825 and becoming known as the Quaker Line because it ran on rails manufactured in Quaker factories. When the Napoleonic Wars broke out, these Quaker businesses put their pacifist beliefs into practice and declined to use the factories for the manufacture of cannons, instead of which they diversified into making a vast range of iron products for the domestic market.

In pharmaceutical production, Allen and Hanbury's trace their origins to a partnership of Quaker apothecaries which began in 1715; Bryant & May matches, and the biscuit firms of Huntley & Palmers and Carrs were other companies founded by members of the pacifist group. Think of chocolate manufacture and all the greats were from Quaker backgrounds – the Cadbury's, the Fry's, the Rowntree's – and all of these date their origins back to the Georgian era. And with all of them, female equality meant that women had a voice in the way those companies were run and managed. Quakers were, by and large, anti-war, anti-slavery and anti-capital punishment; they were (and are) pro prison reform, welfare for the poor, and the promotion of the education of girls as well as boys.

Surprising for a faith opposed to the evils of the demon drink, the Quakers were also prominent brewers, feeling that it was the lesser of two evils to encourage people to drink beer rather than wines and spirits. It is interesting to look at the salutary story of the Thrales. Here was a family with a long tradition of brewing beer in the capital. Henry Thrale, a long-time friend of Samuel Johnson, developed the business throughout the middle years of the eighteenth century, but when he died in 1781 his widow Hester and their (mostly female) children were far more interested in being fashionable and in being seen at all the right places. They spent money like water and almost bankrupted the company. At that point, fate intervened. As Hester later wrote: 'God Almighty sent us a knot of rich Quakers.' She sold the business for £135,000 and at last Hester was restored 'to my original rank in life and a situation undisturbed by commercial jargon, undisgraced by commercial connexion'. The wording is interesting: in her eyes, 'trade' for a woman was a disgraceful thing, something to be avoided or kept quiet about. It was certainly a snobbish time. No one 'in trade' would ever have been allowed through the doors of fashionable clubs and assemblies such as Almacks. Women, in particular, played down their involvement in businesses, hiding their reputations behind the names of dead husbands or of ineffectual sons.

These achievements are all the more remarkable given that Quakers only accounted for little over one tenth of 1 per cent of the population. They were amongst the first to set a firm price for goods. Other traders would haggle, but the Quakers refused to do this, insisting on 'a fair price for a decent product'. They established a reputation for honesty and integrity, and this was no accident. The Quaker community did not regard it as sufficient that a business was run profitably; it had to be run in an ethical manner. Meetings would be held within the Quaker community, attended both by men and by women, where business ethics would be discussed. They also offered a support network to fellow Quakers and there were far fewer failures of Quaker banks and Quaker businesses in the eighteenth century, compared to the rest of the marketplace. This in turn reflects the close network of Quaker families. If a businessman died, his widow would lend any money she had to provide capital to other younger entrepreneurs. This network was strengthened by the Quaker rule that members could only marry within their own faith, and endogamous marriages were the norm until as late as 1860. Not only that, but Quaker committees would scrutinise the marriage proposal and make sure that the pair were living their lives in accordance with Quaker values. Quite simply, being a Quaker was not something you did on a Sunday: it was a lifestyle, seven days a week.

But if the Quakers were a minority group who 'punched above their weight', how come their ideas on equality failed to sweep away gender inequality in the nineteenth century, as it had started to do in the previous hundred years? The answer has to be that Victorian prudery, their love of 'appearances', modesty and the view that women had their own sphere of influence, i.e. in the home, simply swamped any genuine move towards equality.

Was it simply a case that men ganged up on women to protect 'their' territory and to keep women chained to the kitchen sink, or was it that women chose not to aspire to equality, and preferred to stay at home? There is of course no single answer. Lack of education for women obviously held back many who might otherwise have achieved academic success, or gone on to careers in medicine, science, and so on.

It is often suggested that the concept of 'separate spheres' meant that women were happy having dominion in the private sphere – the idea of the 'Angel of the Hearth' in charge of running the home and looking after the children, leaving men free to excel in the public sphere. It is however an idea which sits somewhat unhappily with the fact that in 1837 Victoria came to the throne, the first female monarch for 123 years. Surely, if ever there was a time when women would have sought to emulate their leader by showing that they too could fulfil a role in government, in public affairs, as leaders and visionaries, it was in 1837. Absurdly, the invisible barrier remained. And isn't it strange that when men were faced with a queen who was ruler of the largest empire the world had ever known, a land where the sun never set on the British Empire, they chose to slam the door shut on the idea of women being treated as equals in the business world?

Perhaps more than anything else, the early attempts at a move towards equality received a massive setback in the aftermath of the French Revolution. Here, for all to see, was what could happen if 'change for the sake of change' were permitted. Society recoiled in horror from the lack of order, and ironically Mary Wollstonecraft fed into this once her private life became known to a wider public. People were appalled at her behaviour and in condemning her conduct they effectively banned her ideas from 'decent society'. Instead of leading to change, her ideas were consigned to 100 years in the wilderness. In their place came conformity, tradition, and subordination to men. In fairness to Mary Wollstonecraft she did not seek to spread the message that it was good for women to have affairs, or to have children out of wedlock, but those were the headline stories from her life which people judged her by, and those ideas were simply too revolutionary for their time. She fuelled a backlash, and set the women's movement back by many years. Into that void, male bigotry and prejudice seemed to flourish as never before.

That is not to say that there were no further attempts in the Georgian era to advance the cause of women. In 1825 William Thompson and his partner Anna Wheeler published an *Appeal of One Half the Human Race, Women, Against the Pretensions of the Other Half, Men* and for perhaps the first time, eloquently set out the case for extending full political rights to all women. Their case was that getting rid of the restrictions would be for the greater good of all society.

A growing realisation that men should not automatically be given custody of children led to the Infants Custody Act in 1839. This gave a mother custody rights in respect of all children under the age of 7, provided that she was 'of good character'. However, the concept that questions about custody should involve looking at what was in the best interests of the child did not gain support until a later century. Other campaigns led to the Married Women's Property Act, eventually passed in 1882, but again this was only the first of a great many steps towards equal rights on marriage and divorce.

Men no doubt thought women were their own worst enemy, and it is certainly true that male arrogance and narrow-mindedness helped enshrine female lack of status and reputation. As long ago as 1731 'Sophia', the anonymous author of *Women not inferior to men*, was writing, 'Why is learning useless to us? Because we have no share in public office. And why have we no share in public offices? Because we have no learning.'

The same book looks at the success of females occupying the British throne and poses the question:

And since, as we have said, this nation has seen many glorious instances of Women, severally qualified to have all public authority centr'd in them: why may they not be as qualified at least for the subordinate offices of ministers of state, vice-queens, governesses, secretaries, privy counsellors and treasurers? Or why may they not without oddity, be even generals of armies, and admirals of fleets?

Well, the answer to those questions is that it took until 1929 for Margaret Bondfield to become the first female cabinet minister, and the first woman to be a privy counsellor, when she was appointed Minister of Labour in the Labour government of 1929–31. The first female prime minister was Margaret Thatcher in 1979 and this country's first female general was appointed in 2015 when Susan Ridge was promoted to the two-star position of major as Director General Army Legal Services (in charge of a team of 130 lawyers). In 2013 Elaine West was promoted to Air Vice-Marshal – the highest military rank ever held by a woman. Nine years earlier Carolyn J. Stait (now retired) became the first woman to command a Naval Base in Britain when she was appointed commander of HMNB Clyde in Scotland, the home of the UK's nuclear deterrent at the Faslane naval base. She was the first woman to be promoted to the rank of commodore in direct competition with male officers: as of 2016 no woman has held a higher rank in the Royal Navy. 'Sophia' – in reality probably Lady Mary Wortley Montagu, but possibly Lady Sophia Fermor – may have been heard to mutter in her grave, 'Well it's taken long enough…'.

Others can argue whether equality has actually been achieved. The one thing which is apparent is that the move towards equality got going in the eighteenth century and received an enormous boost from the women such as the ones featured in this book; and that this was then followed by a century (and in some cases nearly two centuries) of obstruction, apathy and stagnation. Whatever women achieved in the Georgian era was largely negated by what happened in the Victorian era, with its emphasis on the role of the woman as a homemaker and mother, and it is only recently, very recently, that the pendulum has swung the other way.

***

To put things in perspective, here are a few statistics from the past fifty years or so:

AIRLINE PILOTS: Yvonne Pope Sintes became Britain's first commercial airline captain in 1972, while Captain Lynn Barton became British Airways' first female pilot in 1987. When BA took over British Caledonian in 1987 it employed over 3,000 pilots, but only sixty of them were women and no woman had ever piloted Concorde. Barbara Harmer was chosen to undergo the intensive six-month conversion course and on 25 March 1993 she became the first qualified female Concorde pilot. Later that year she made her first Concorde flight as First Officer to New York City's John F. Kennedy International Airport.

In 2015 the International Society of Women Airline Pilots estimated that there are about 4,000 women pilots worldwide, out of a total of some 130,000. That is just over 3 per cent. Six per cent of EasyJet's flying staff are female, much the same as British Airways, which employs 200 women out of 3,500 pilots.

SURGEONS in the UK: A recent British Medical Journal found that only 10 per cent of surgeons are female, and yet according to UCAS, in 2011 55 per cent of people accepted on to medical degree courses in the UK were women. The increased proportion of female medical students has not, as yet, been translated into a correspondingly increased proportion of women surgeons.

BISHOPS: In January 2015 The Church of England consecrated its first female bishop during a ceremony at York Minster, when The Right Reverend Libby Lane was made Bishop of Stockport.

ASTRONAUTS: As of July 2016, sixty women have flown in space, out of a total of 537 space travellers.

ELECTRICIANS AND PLUMBERS: When did you last see a female one? A recent review of the data relating to women in engineering and technology showed that only 9 per cent of UK engineering professionals are women compared to 18 per cent in Spain, 26 per cent in Sweden and 20 per cent in Italy. A UCATT report in 2016 suggests women make up only 11 per cent of the construction workforce and just 1 per cent of workers on site. The Office for National Statistics says that the number of women working as roofers, bricklayers and glaziers is so low that it is incapable of being measured.

HGV DRIVERS: Only 1.2 per cent of drivers of heavy goods vehicles in the UK are women and it is a similar story across Europe. The United States figures are higher at 5.8 per cent but women are still very much in the minority. Reasons given by women for not becoming HGV drivers include the comment that the toilet and shower facilities are not designed with women in mind....

WOMEN IN PARLIAMENT: 191 women MPs were elected at the 2015 General Election, which equates to 29 per cent of all MPs – and a record high. In the June 2017 election this went up to 32 per cent – a total of 208 female MPs. Prior to 1987 women had never been more than 5 per cent of MPs. In the last 100 years 452 women have been elected to the Commons (five fewer than the number of male MPs in 2015).

MICHELIN-STARRED CHEFS: In the 2012 Michelin guide, listing the best 106 restaurant chefs awarded three stars, only one was a woman. Her name is Anne Sophie Pic and she was the first female chef to be given a rating of three stars by Michelin since 1968. There were roughly 2,500 restaurants that were awarded stars by Michelin. Of those, only ten of them had female chefs. This has to be seen in context of the fact that worldwide there are far more women who learn to cook than men.

POLICE OFFICERS: A Home Office report in 2015 shows that there were 35,738 female police officers in the forty-three police forces on 31 March 2015, representing 28.2 per cent of the total. The proportion of women in senior ranks (i.e. chief inspector and above) was 21.4 per cent.

FTSE 100: In 2016 there are seven female CEOs in the FTSE 100 companies – in other words, 7 per cent.

EDUCATION
IS THE MOST
POWERFUL WEAPON
WE CAN USE TO
CHANGE THE WORLD

Education, then as now, is the key ….

Appendix

The Education of Women
by Daniel Defoe

I have often thought of it as one of the most barbarous customs in the world, considering us as a civilised and a Christian country, that we deny the advantages of learning to women. We reproach the sex every day with folly and impertinence; while I am confident, had they the advantages of education equal to us, they would be guilty of less than ourselves.

One would wonder, indeed, how it should happen that women are conversible at all; since they are only beholden to natural parts, for all their knowledge. Their youth is spent to teach them to stitch and sew or make baubles. They are taught to read, indeed, and perhaps to write their names, or so; and that is the height of a woman's education. And I would but ask any who slight the sex for their understanding, what is a man (a gentleman, I mean) good for, that is taught no more? I need not give instances, or examine the character of a gentleman, with a good estate, or a good family, and with tolerable parts; and examine what figure he makes for want of education.

The soul is placed in the body like a rough diamond; and must be polished, or the lustre of it will never appear. And 'tis manifest, that as the rational soul distinguishes us from brutes; so education carries on the distinction, and makes some less brutish than others. This is too evident to need any demonstration. But why then should women be denied the benefit of instruction? If knowledge and understanding had been useless additions to the sex, God Almighty would never have given them capacities; for he made nothing needless. Besides, I would ask such, what they can see in ignorance, that they should think it a necessary ornament to a woman? or how much worse is a wise woman than a fool? or what has the woman done to forfeit the privilege of being taught? Does she plague us with her pride and impertinence? Why did we not let her learn, that she might have had more wit? Shall we upbraid women with folly, when 'tis only the error of this inhuman custom, that hindered them from being made wiser?

The capacities of women are supposed to be greater, and their senses quicker than those of the men; and what they might be capable of being bred to, is plain from some instances of female wit, which this age is not without. Which upbraids us with Injustice, and looks as if we denied women the advantages of education, for fear they should vie with the men in their improvements....

[They] should be taught all sorts of breeding suitable both to their genius and quality. And in particular, Music and Dancing; which it would be cruelty to bar the sex of, because they are their darlings. But besides this, they should be taught languages, as particularly French and Italian: and I would venture the injury of giving a woman more tongues than one. They should, as a particular study, be taught all the graces of speech, and all the necessary air of conversation; which our common education is so defective in, that I need not expose it. They should be brought to read books, and especially history; and so to read as to make them understand the world, and be able to know and judge of things when they hear of them.

To such whose genius would lead them to it, I would deny no sort of learning; but the chief thing, in general, is to cultivate the understandings of the sex, that they may be capable of all sorts of conversation; that their parts and judgements being improved, they may be as profitable in their conversation as they are pleasant.

Women, in my observation, have little or no difference in them, but as they are or are not distinguished by education. Tempers, indeed, may in some degree influence them, but the main distinguishing part is their Breeding.

The whole sex are generally quick and sharp. I believe, I may be allowed to say, generally so: for you rarely see them lumpish and heavy, when they are children; as boys will often be. If a woman be well bred, and taught the proper management of her natural wit, she proves generally very sensible and retentive.

And, without partiality, a woman of sense and manners is the finest and most delicate part of God's Creation, the glory of Her Maker, and the great instance of His singular regard to man, His darling creature: to whom He gave the best gift either God could bestow or man receive. And 'tis the sordidest piece of folly and ingratitude in the world, to withhold from the sex the due lustre which the advantages of education gives to the natural beauty of their minds.

A woman well bred and well taught, furnished with the additional accomplishments of knowledge and behaviour, is a creature without comparison. Her society is the emblem of sublimer enjoyments, her person is angelic, and her conversation heavenly. She is all softness and sweetness, peace, love, wit, and delight. She is every way suitable to the sublimest wish, and the man that has such a one to his portion, has nothing to do but to rejoice in her, and be thankful.

On the other hand, Suppose her to be the very same woman, and rob her of the benefit of education, and it follows

If her temper be good, want of education makes her soft and easy.

Her wit, for want of teaching, makes her impertinent and talkative.

Her knowledge, for want of judgement and experience, makes her fanciful and whimsical.

If her temper be bad, want of breeding makes her worse; and she grows haughty, Insolent, and loud.

If she be passionate, want of manners makes her a termagant and a scold, which is much at one with Lunatic.

If she be proud, want of discretion (which still is breeding) makes her conceited, fantastic, and ridiculous.

And from these she degenerates to be turbulent, clamorous, noisy, nasty, the devil!

The great distinguishing difference, which is seen in the world between men and women, is in their education; and this is manifested by comparing it with the difference between one man or woman, and another.

And herein it is that I take upon me to make such a bold assertion, That all the world are mistaken in their practice about women. For I cannot think that God Almighty ever made them so delicate, so glorious creatures; and furnished them with such charms, so agreeable and so delightful to mankind; with souls capable of the same accomplishments with men: and all, to be only Stewards of our Houses, Cooks, and Slaves.

Not that I am for exalting the female government in the least: but, in short, I would have men take women for companions, and educate them to be fit for it. A woman of sense and breeding will scorn as much to encroach upon the prerogative of man, as a man of sense will scorn to oppress the weakness of the woman. But if the women's souls were refined and improved by teaching, that word would be lost. To say, the weakness of the sex, as to judgment, would be nonsense; for ignorance and folly would be no more to be found among women than men.

I remember a passage, which I heard from a very fine woman. She had wit and capacity enough, an extraordinary shape and face, and a great fortune: but had been cloistered up all her time; and for fear of being stolen, had not had the liberty of being taught the common necessary knowledge of women's affairs. And when she came to converse in the world, her natural wit made her so sensible of the want of education, that she gave this short reflection on herself: "I am ashamed to talk with my very maids," says she, "for I don't know when they do right or wrong. I had more need go to school, than be married."

I need not enlarge on the loss the defect of education is to the sex; nor argue the benefit of the contrary practice. 'Tis a thing will be more easily granted than remedied. This chapter is but an Essay at the thing: and I refer the Practice to those Happy Days (if ever they shall be) when men shall be wise enough to mend it.

Boarding School Education – or the Frenchified Young Lady.

Bibliography

Archenholz, Johan Wilhelm von: *A Picture of England* London, 1789. Available in digitised form via Internet Archive at https://archive.org/details/apictureengland00archgoog

Austen, Jane: *Pride & Prejudice* London 1813.

Bentham, Jeremy: *Works* London, 1843. Ed. John Bowring. Via Online Library of Liberty at http://oll.libertyfund.org/titles/1920.

Blackstone, William: *Commentaries on the Laws of England* London, Clarendon Press 1765-79. Available online via Yale Law School at http://avalon.law.yale.edu/ subject_menus/blackstone.asp

Burney, Fanny: *Evelina – or the History of a Young Lady's Entrance into the World* London, Penguin Classics 1994.

Burney, Fanny: *Cecilia – or the Memoirs of an Heiress* London, Oxford World's Classics 1988.

Burney, Fanny: *Camilla – or a Picture of Youth* London, Oxford World's Classics 1983.

Bunyan, John: *The Pilgrim's Progress* London, 1678 (more accessibly, as a version edited by R. Sharrock and J. B. Wharey. (Oxford: Oxford University Press, 1975).

Byrne, Richard: *Prisons and Punishments of London* Harper Collins, 1992.

Campbell, R: *The London Tradesman: Being a Compendious View of All the Trades* London, T Gardner, 1747. (https://books.google.es/books?id=nNoHAAAAQAAJ&redir_esc=y)

Chalus, Elaine and Hannah Barker: *Gender in Eighteenth-Century England* London, Longman, 1997.

Chapone, Hester: *Letters on the Improvement of the Mind* London, 1773.

Corry, John: *A satirical View of London – comprehending a Sketch of Manners of the Age* London, 1803. Available via University of Harvard at http://catalog.hathitrust.org/ Record/009710618

Crawford and Mendelson: *Women in Early Modern England 1550-1720* London, Clarendon Press, 1998.

Darwin, Erasmus: *Plan for the Conduct of Female Education in Boarding Schools* London, J. Johnson, 1797.

Defoe, Daniel: *The Education of Women* London, 1719. Available online at http:// www.bartleby.com/27/13.html

Defoe, Daniel: *A Tour thro' the Whole Island of Great Britain* London, 1724. Available online at https://archive.org/stream/tourthroughthew006736mbp/tourthroughtthew006736mbp_djvu.txt

Defoe, Daniel: *Roxana – the fortunate Mistress* London, 1724. Oxford University Press, 1996.

Defoe, Daniel: *Complete English Tradesman* London, 1726. Available in digital format at: http://www.gutenberg.org/files/14444/14444-h/14444-h.htm

Erickson, Amy Louise: *Clockmakers, Milliners and Mistresses: Women Trading in the City of London Companies 1700-1750* Available online via http://www.geog.cam.ac.uk/research/projects/occupations/abstracts/paper16.pdf

Erickson, Amy Louise: *Mistresses and marriage: or, a short history of the Mrs.* Cambridge University Research Project, available on-line at http://www.geog.cam.ac.uk/research/projects/occupations/abstracts/paper25.pdf

Fordyce, James: *Sermons to Young Women* London, 1766. Available on-line via the British Library at http://www.bl.uk/collection-items/sermons-to-young-women

Foster & Cordell: *Chilies to Chocolate: Food the Americas Gave the World* Tucson, University of Arizona Press, 1992.

Fry, K. and R. E. Cresswell: *Memoir of the life of Elizabeth Fry, with extracts from her journal and letters* London, John Hatchard & Co 1847. Available online via Harvard University at https://archive.org/stream/memoirlifeeliza06cresgoog#page/n10/mode/2up

Gisborne, Thomas: *An Enquiry into the Duties of the Female Sex* London 1797. Available online at https://archive.org/details/anenquiryintodu02gisbgoog

Glasse, Hannah: *The Art of Cookery made Plain and Easy* London, 1747. Available online at https://books.google.es/books?id=xJdAAAAAIAAJ

Godwin, William: *Memoirs of the Author of A Vindication of the Rights of Woman* London, Joseph Johnson, 1798. Available online at http://www.gutenberg.org/ebooks/16199

Gross, Jonathan David: *The Life of Anne Damer: Portrait of a Regency Artist* Plymouth, Lexington Books, 2014.

Harman, Claire: *Fanny Burney, a biography* London, Harper Collins, 2000.

Heller, Deborah: *Bluestockings Now! – The Evolution of a Social Role* London, Ashgate Publishing, 2015.

Hunt, Margaret: *Women and the Enlightenment* The Haworth Press, 1984.

Manvell, Roger: *Sarah Siddons, Portrait of an Actress* London, William Heinemann Ltd 1970.

McCreery, Cindy: *The Satirical Gaze: Prints of Women in Late Eighteenth-century England* Clarendon Press, 2004.

More, Hannah; *Search after Happiness* Bristol: S. Farley, 1773.

More, Hannah; *Essays on Various Subjects, Principally Designed for Young Ladies* London 1777 (available in digital format at https://archive.org/details/essaysonvariouss00more)

More, Hannah; *Village Politics, by Will Chip* London, 1792.

More, Hannah: *Strictures on the Modern System of Female Education With a View of the Principles and Conduct Prevalent Among Women of Rank and Fortune* London, T. Cadell and W. Davies 1799 (available in digital format at http://digital.library.lse.ac.uk/objects/lse:gis329lag

More, Hannah; *Coelebs in Search of a Wife* London, 1801.

Nichols, John: *The Gentleman's Magazine* London, E. Cave 1736-1850. Available online from Hathi Trust Digital Library at http://catalog.hathitrust.org/Record/006056643

Olsen, Kirstin: *Daily Life in 18th-century England* Santa Barbara, Greenwood Publishing Group, 1999.

Oxford Dictionary of National Biography Oxford University Press 2004. Online version available on subscription at http://www.oxforddnb.com

Polkinghorn, Bette: *Jane Marcet: An Uncommon Woman* Berkshire, Forestwood Publications, 1993.

Polwele, Richard: *The Unsex'd Females, a Poem* Cadell and Davies, London, 1798.

Pope, Alexander: *The Dunciad*. London, 1728. (Available as an e-book at https://ebooks.adelaide.edu.au/p/pope/alexander/dunciad/complete.html)

Radzinowicz, Leon: *A History of English Criminal Law and Its Administration from 1750* London, Stevens and Sons, 1948. Available online at: http://www.jstor.org/stable/4503799?seq=1#page_scan_tab_contents

Raffald, Elizabeth: *The Experienced English Housekeeper* Manchester, J. Harrop, 1769. Tenth edition available via Internet Archive at https://archive.org/details/experiencedengl00raffgoog

Roberts, William: *Memoirs of the life and correspondence of Mrs Hannah More* New York. Harper, 1835.

Scott, Simon: *Artificial Stone: A Successful Substitute for Natural Stone?* Northampton, Haddonstone Ltd, 2009.

Sharp, Jane, *The Midwives Book; or, The Whole Art of Midwifery Discovered*. London 1671.

Sharpe, Pamela: *Women's Work: The English Experience 1650-1914*. New York: Oxford University Press Inc., 1998.

Shure, David: *Hester Bateman – Queen of English Silversmiths* New York, Doubleday, 1959.

Simonton, Deborah: *The Routledge History of Women in Europe since 1700* Abingdon, Routledge, 2006.

'Sophia': *Women not inferior to men.* John Hawkins, London, 1731. Available in digital format at: http://digital.library.upenn.edu/women/sophia/woman/woman.html

Stone, Sarah: *A Complete Practice of Midwifery.* T. Cooper, London, 1737.

The Georgian Era – Memoirs of the most eminent persons who have flourished …. Vizetelly, Branston & Co, London, 1834. Available in digital format at https://archive.org/details/georgianeramemoi04clar

Thompson, Lynda M: *The 'scandalous Memoirists': Constantia Phillips, Laetitia Pilkington and the shame of publick fame* Manchester, Manchester University Press, 2000.

Thompson, William and Anna Wheeler: *Appeal of one Half of the Human Race, Women, against the Pretensions of the other Half, Men …* Longmans, London, 1825 and available online at http://digital.library.lse.ac.uk/objects/lse:cik442nul

Unkel, Jill: *Wicked Wit – Darly's comic prints* Dublin, Chester Beatty Library, 2015.

Walker, Joseph Cooper: *Hints for a System of Education for a Female Orphan House* Dublin, 1793. Available online via LSE Digital Library at http://digital.library.lse.ac.uk/objects/lse:wof874yey

Williams, Gareth: *Angel of Death – the story of Smallpox* Palgrave Macmillan, 2010.

Wilson, Kathleen: *The Island Race: Englishness, Empire and Gender in the Eighteenth Century* New York, Routledge, 2003.

Wollstonecraft, Mary: *Thoughts on the Education of Daughters: with Reflections on Female Conduct in the more important Duties of Life* London, Joseph Johnson, 1787. Available online at http://digital.library.lse.ac.uk/objects/lse:ruf494jak?id=lse%3Aruf494jak#page/172/mode/2up

Wollstonecraft, Mary: *A Vindication of the Rights of Woman: with Strictures on Political and Moral Subjects* London, Joseph Johnson, 1792. Also available online at http://www.gutenberg.org/ebooks/3420

Wollstonecraft, Mary: *Letters Written during a Short Residence in Sweden, Norway, and Denmark* London, Joseph Johnson, 1796. Also available online at http://www.gutenberg.org/files/3529/3529-h/3529-h.htm

Wortley Montagu, Mary: *Letters from Turkey,* 1763 London (available as an e-book at https://ebooks.adelaide.edu.au/m/montagu/mary_wortley/letters/index.html)

Yearsley, Ann: *Poems, on Several Occasions* London, Cadell, 1785.

Image accreditation

A sincere thanks to all who have made images available for use in this book – it is really appreciated.

Text images
Page viii, Image 1: 'Washerwomen' by Paul Sandby. Yale Center for British Art B1977.14.5133.

Page xx, Image 2: 'The Ladies Waldegrave' by Valentine Green, after Sir Joshua Reynolds. Mezzotint, published 1781. National Portrait Gallery. NPG D37981.

Page 1, Image 3: Comedy and tragedy mask.

Page 9, Image 4: 'Two Girls Seated' by Paul Sandby. Yale Center for British Art, B2001.2.1168.

Page 17, Image 5: 'London Cries' by Paul Sandby, Yale Center for British Art B1975.3.209.

Page 27, Image 6: Sarah Siddons paper cut-out by Auguste Edouart, 1832. National Portrait Gallery, NPG D396.

Page 29, Image 7: Extract from trade card for John Bird, mathematical instrument maker. Lewis Walpole Library, lwlpr21026.

Page 37, Image 8: Diary extracts by Richard Hall – author's private collection.

Page 46, Image 9: Thomas Rowlandson's 'Still Tickling is Butt Teasing' 1825. Chris Beetles Gallery.

Page 53, Image 10: Proof 'Cartwheel' Two pence, Soho Mint, Birmingham. © Birmingham Museums and Art Gallery.

Page 69, Image 11: 'Modern Hospitality – or A Friendly Party in High Life' by James Gillray showing Lady Archer fleecing the Prince Regent at Faro. Metropolitan Museum of Modern Art. Accession Number: 42.121(18).

Page 75, Image 12: William Hogarth's 'Five Orders of Periwigs', 1761. Lewis Walpole Library, lwlpr22653.

Page 83, Image 13: M Darly's 'The Macaroni Printseller', 1772. Lewis Walpole Library, lwlpr03343.

Page 88, Image 14: 'The Story of Pamela', plate 9, engraved by L. Truchy after a painting by Joseph Highmore, London, England, 1745. From the collections of the Colonial Williamsburg Foundation.

Page 95, Image 15: 'A Milliner's Shop', by Henry Kingsbury, 1787. Lewis Walpole Library, lwlpr787.03.24.01.

Page 99, Image 16: 'The Quaker Meeting' (public domain).

Page 101, Image 17: 'A curtain lecture!' Etched by Thomas Rowlandson. Lewis Walpole Library, lwlpr09576.

Page 108, Image 18: 'Mrs Montagu' by Wilson Lowry.

Page 113, Image 19: Paper cut-out of Hannah More by Auguste Edouart, 1827; National Portrait Gallery.

Page 121, Image 20: Eighteenth-century Chamberlain's Key, Metropolitan Museum of Modern Art. Accession Number 87.11.637.

Page 129, Image 21: Extract from front page of Mary Wollstonecraft's 'A Vindication of the Rights of Woman', 1792.

Page 141, Image 22: 'Education is the most powerful weapon' – quotation by Nelson Mandela.

Page 145, Image 23: 'Boarding School Education – or the Frenchified Young Lady'. Lewis Walpole Library, lwlpr03170.

Plates

Plate 1: *Fanny Burney* (otherwise Frances d'Arblay) by Edward Francisco Burney, 1784/5. © National Portrait Gallery, London. NPG 2634.

Plate 2: *Lady Reading the Letters of Heloise and Abelard*, by Auguste Bernard d'Agesci (after Greuze). Chicago Institute of Art.

Plate 3: *Mrs Damer* by R Cosway. Lewis Walpole Library, lwlpr15749.

Plate 4: *Miss Siddons*. Undated print made by Peltro W. Tomkins, after John Downman, shown courtesy of the Yale Center for British Art. Accession number B1970.3.514.

Plate 5a: *Lady Mary Wortley Montagu* by Achille Devéria, © National Portrait Gallery, London. NPG D34619.

Plate 5b: *The cow pock – or – the wonderful effects of the new inoculation!* by James Gillray, 1801. © National Portrait Gallery, London. NPG D13037.

Plate 6a: *A Man Mid–Wife*, after Isaac Cruikshank, 1795. Lewis Walpole Library, lwlpr08422.

Plate 6b: Lion on Westminster Bridge, made from coade-stone. Public Domain, https://commons.wikimedia.org/w/index.php?curid=4413389

Plate 7a: Trade Card of Catherine West. Lewis Walpole Library, lwlpr19449.

Plate 7b: Trade Card of Jane Batch. Lewis Walpole Library, lwlpr19409.

Plate 7c: Trade Card of Mrs Campbell. Lewis Walpole Library, lwlpr20755.

Plate 7d: Trade Card of Esther Sleepe. Lewis Walpole Library, lwlpr19411.

Plate 8a: *The Caricature Shop*, by P. Roberts. Lewis Walpole Library lwlpr10184.

Plate 8b: *Two-penny Whist* by James Gillray. Lewis Walpole Library lwlpr08712.

Plate 9a: *Elizabeth Raffald* by an unknown artist, c.1790, © National Portrait Gallery, London. NPG D5574.

Plate 9b: Thomas Rowlandson's *Breaking up of the Blue Stocking Club*. Lewis Walpole Library, lwlpr11823.

Plate 10: *Hannah More* by Henry William Pickersgill. © National Portrait Gallery, London. NPG 412.

Plate 11: Mary Wollstonecraft after John Opie. Library of Congress.

Plate 12a: *Virgin shape Warehouse* by Chares Ansell, 1799. Lewis Walpole Library, lwlpr09557.

Plate 12b: *The Bum Shop* by R. Rushworth, 1785. Lewis Walpole Library, lwlpr05790.

Plate 13a: *Six Stages of mending a face* by Thomas Rowlandson 1792. Lewis Walpole Library, lwlpr07475.

Plate 13b: *Billingsgate Brutes* by Thomas Rowlandson, 1789. Lewis Walpole Library, lwlpr06709.

Plate 14: *The Elopement* by Thomas Rowlandson, 1792. Yale Center for British Art, B1977.14.346.

Plate 15a: *The Boarding School Hairdresser.* Lewis Walpole Library, lwlpr06066.

Plate 15b: *Domestick amusement: The lovely spinner* by James Watson. Lewis Walpole Library, lwlpr02415.

Plate 16a: *Domestick amusement: The fair seamstress* by James Watson. Lewis Walpole Library, lwlpr02414.

Plate 16b: *Domestick Employment – Ironing* by Henry Robert Morland. Yale Center for British Art, Paul Mellon Collection. B1977.14.12021.

My grateful thanks to all the institutions mentioned above for allowing the use of these images.

Index

Livery Companies, 63–5

Marcet, Jane, **38–45**, 131
Middleton, Margaret, 102–107, 111, 131
Midwifery, 51, 90
More, Hannah, 22, 44, 65, 102, 106, **109–13**
    122, 131, 133

Nutt, Elizabeth, 81 – 2

Phillips, Theresia, **84–7**, 134
Pinney, Hesther, **54–9**
Primogeniture, xiv
Pope, Alexander, xvii, 31, 34

Raffald, Elizabeth, **89–94**
Ramsay, James, 104–106
Reynolds, Joshua, 6, 8, 14, 23, 38, 103,
    110, 130

Quakers, *see* Society of Friends

Seward, Anna, 134
Siddons, Sarah, 7, 13, **18–27**
Society of Friends, 44, 96–9, 106, 114, 119,
    130, 135–7
Sommerville, Mary, 45

Telford, Thomas, 49
Trade cards, x, 64, 133
Walpole, Horace, 11–14, 35, 76, 77,
    111, 122

Wedgwood, Sally, 134
Wilberforce, William, 102, 105, 111
Wilbraham, Elizabeth, 131
Wollstonecraft, Mary, 4, 44, 111, **122–9**
Wortley Montagu, Lady Mary, **30–7**, 42, 139
Wright, Patricia, 16, 66